Dowsing
Techniques and Applications

Tom Graves

Turnstone Books

Turnstone Books
37 Upper Addison Gardens
London W14

© copyright 1976 Tom Graves

Paperback ISBN 0 85500 057 0
Hardback ISBN 0 85500 066 X

First published 1976
Second impression March 1977

Printed and bound in Great Britain by
Eyre and Spottiswoode Ltd, Grosvenor Press, Portsmouth,
Hants

To Jan

Contents

Acknowledgements

This book is the result of many years' avid collection of apparently useless information, and of meeting over the years the many people who gave that useless information its use. In a way everyone I've ever met must have been involved in the process, but in particular I'd like to thank my mother, who always taught me to question; my wife, who proof-read and put up with the whole crazy project; Bill Lewis and John Williams, dowsers of Abergavenny, who got me to *do* it instead of theorizing about it; the staff of the Visual Research department at Hornsey College of Art, and Professor Christopher Cornford and Bernard Myers of the Royal College of Art, who almost unknowingly helped me with much of the theoretical and structural side of my research; the staff and students of the various places I've studied and taught; and Alick Bartholomew at Turnstone, who nursemaided this book from a woolly idea to what you're holding now.

PART ONE

A Practical Introduction

1 By way of introduction

Anyone can dowse. It's just a skill which, like any other, can be learnt with practice, awareness and a working knowledge of its basic principles and mechanics – a skill which you can use as and when you need. At any stage within it you need some kind of instrument and at least a rough idea of how to use it; you need to have some idea of what you're looking for and how to go about looking for it; and you need to know when you've found it. But there's nothing complicated in that: you can make most types of instrument yourself for a few pence, and the techniques – once shorn of their many layers of empirical confusion – turn out to be surprisingly simple, even if not quite compatible with the lifeless materialistic philosophies of the present day.

But for reasons which should become clear as I go along, I don't intend to present a theory of dowsing here. Neither do I wish to write a history of the subject, for other writers have already written more than adequate histories. What concerns me here is the *practice* of dowsing: how to learn it, and how to learn to *use* it.

In talking of use, though, I feel it's a mistake to define dowsing in terms of its uses, its applications – there's far more to it than water-divining, medical dowsing or my own speciality of 'live' archaeology. Equally, there's more to it than its techniques, whether they be traditional techniques for finding minerals, or the more recent and bizarre techniques of map-dowsing and time-dowsing. Dowsing is more than a subject, it's a skill, a tool – one which I suppose can be used to tackle any problem you care to name.

In another sense it's not so much a subject as a specific state of mind: it's a *mental* tool, in that it appears to be an analytical tool which uses intuition, an intuitive tool based on analysis, and both of these put together – a paradoxical mental tool! A useful one, though, for it fits neatly into the awkward gap between the 'thinking' tools of logic, analysis and 'scientific method', and the 'feeling' tools of imagination, intuition and 'subjective meaning'. But like all tools dowsing has a purpose, a set of uses – mental uses – and while you *can* use it to tackle any problem you'll find that in many situations (especially the more 'ordinary' ones) other tools are more useful. Dowsing isn't a panacea for all the world's ills – as some writers seem to imply – nor is it infallible; but if you use it intelligently you'll soon find just how useful it can be.

Being somewhat subjective it's also personal, and so you'll find that every dowser – including you – develops his or her own way of doing things. Although some of the techniques I'll be describing here are traditional, and others are gratefully borrowed from friends, most are based on my own experience and interpretation. So beware – this book is full of personal opinions!

Not that there's anything wrong in that, of course. But do keep that in mind when reading and using this book, so that you don't make the all-too-common blunder of mistaking opinions for immutable 'facts'. Above all, *don't* mistake my various statements for theory, for I know of few quicker ways of getting into intellectual knots than trying to theorize about causes and mechanisms in dowsing. It only makes sense in practice.

But because this is a practical subject I've had to structure this book in a slightly unusual way. This has to be not only a manual on the mechanics of dowsing, but also in some ways a manual on the use of you. So the book is in three parts – three courses of the same meal, if you like. The first part is a practical introduction, intended to give you some immediate experience of dowsing and, like *hors d'oeuvres*, to whet your appetite and stimulate the awareness of your senses. The second is the main course – a range of techniques: I may have had to skimp a bit here and there, but it should provide a balanced diet, solid, and with enough of everything that's needed for the work you want to do. And the third course is the pudding – a brief look at some applications of dowsing – in which the proof of the subject, of course, is in the eating.

Like any good meal, you'll miss most of its flavour if you rush it – so take it slowly, take your time. Like any unfamiliar dish, you won't *know* if you like it (or dislike it) until you've tried it yourself – so try out the ideas in practice, not in theory. And note that you will have to use a little ingenuity, a little observation and a little 'common sense' to convert my descriptions and feelings into *your* experience and *your* sense of practice.

And this brings me to the last point of this introduction, which is that neither I, nor anyone else, can *teach* you to dowse: the most anyone can do is to help you to learn. True, I can give you some background information, and some encouragement, in this easily-digestible three-course-meal of a book; I can lend you some of my experience; but that's about all I can do. The rest is up to you. So if you're not particularly interested at the moment, leave it till some other time; but if you want to try it for yourself, read on, and start 'eating'!

2 Down to work

The great mistake people will make when studying dowsing – or any practical subject, for that matter – is to learn *about* it instead of learning it. I made that mistake myself. I spent years reading about the theory of dowsing and getting confused by the various writers' conflicting and self-contradictory statements, before it dawned on me that the way to learn it was to go out and do it. Practice has to come first; theory comes later, when you're trying to work out what has happened!

So let's go straight into practice. The first thing you need is some kind of instrument, and also some idea of what to do with it. Most dowsing reactions show themselves as small movements of the hands – movements often too small to be seen or felt – and so dowsers use a variety of instruments as mechanical amplifiers to make these movements more obvious. Most of these 'mechanical amplifiers' are simple enough to be made in a matter of minutes from things lying around at home: the type I'd like you to start on – 'angle rods' – consists of two pieces of bent wire.

Making angle rods To be more precise, the 'two bent wires' can be made out of any material you care to use, but the easiest way to make the rods is to cut up a pair of old wire coat-hangers. Take one of these and cut the bottom rail at one end with a pair of pliers or wire-cutters. Cut the opposite arm about five inches up from the bend, so that the hanger is in two pieces. Dispose of the part with the hook – it's the part with the bottom rail that you want. Bend the short arm of this part back at a right-angle to the bottom rail. (Stick a piece of tape, or something similar, on each

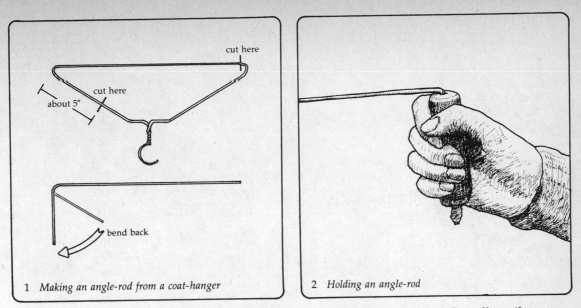

<table>
<tr><td>1 Making an angle-rod from a coat-hanger</td><td>2 Holding an angle-rod</td></tr>
</table>

end of the rod, by the way, or you may accidentally spike some-one's eye with the sharp points.) Now cut up the other hanger in the same way. The two L-shaped rods you should now have are your angle rods.

Holding the rods The short arm of each L is the part you hold: it should be held in a loosely clenched fist. At least, that's the simplest way, though I generally prefer to use some kind of sleeves for the short arms to turn in. I use short lengths of thin tubing, or else dowelling with a small hole bored down the middle – but a stack of two or three cotton reels for each rod will do just as well. Either way, the idea is that the rods can swing freely from side to side, and hence the need for *loosely* clenched fists or for the sleeves.

So take a rod – with or without a sleeve – in each hand. Let your arms hang limp by your sides for a moment, and just relax. This is important – just why I'll explain later. Now bring your arms up so that the rods are roughly horizontal. Keep your wrists well apart, say about body-width: if you bring them close

3 *Working position of angle rods*

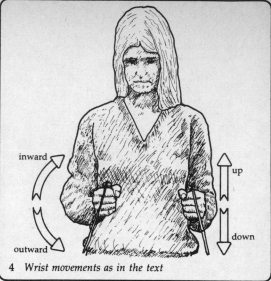

4 *Wrist movements as in the text*

together and tuck your elbows in you'll cramp yourself, which won't help. When you've done this the long arms of the rods should be pointing away from you and roughly parallel to each other. This is their working or 'neutral' position.

The rods' movements Before you start on any practical exercises it would be a good idea to look at what the rods do. Note that it's your wrists, or more precisely your wrist-movements, that do the 'doing', the moving. The rods, being held in a simple balance by your hands, will respond to any movements your wrists might make, but even though it may (and indeed should) feel like it at times, they cannot move of their own accord. So first twist your wrists slightly inwards in a vertical plane: both rods will swing inwards and cross over. If you reverse the movement both rods will swing outwards, and if you twist both wrists in the same direction both rods should swing, roughly parallel, to point in the same direction. And though that's about all that the rods can do, you'll see later just how much you can tell from these three reactions.

The other point you should note is that the nearer you hold the long arms of the rods to the horizontal, the more sensitive will they be to those twisting movements. Tilt the rods downwards a little – say ten or fifteen degrees from the horizontal – and twist your wrists to get the rods to swing as above. Note how much you have to twist to get the rods to cross over. Now hold the rods nearly horizontal, and you'll see that you only have to twist your wrists a small amount to get the same degree of cross-over. If you tilt the rods too far up though, you'll find it difficult to keep them in the 'neutral' position – so find for yourself an angle at which you can keep them stable.

A matter of balance
Holding the 'neutral' position of the rods will seem fairly easy when you're sitting or standing still; but it's quite another matter to hold them in that position when you're walking along. If you allow the rods to sway about all over the place, you won't be able to tell if they're reacting to something interesting or only to your own lack of balance. So the first exercise is to learn how to handle the rods in practice, how to maintain a fairly stable 'neutral', and generally to see what happens when you use the rods in practice.

● Get up out of your armchair and relax for a moment before holding the rods in the 'neutral' position.

● See if you can maintain that 'neutral' while walking along. Do this indoors or outdoors – either will do. Relax: *don't* try to force the rods to remain stable by rigidly clamping your hands, as you'll find that only makes things worse. The trick here is to watch the tips of the rods and rest your mind, so to speak, on the *idea* of the rods remaining parallel. Just relax and let your eyes, your hands and the rods sort it out themselves.

● Strike a balance between holding the 'neutral' and letting the rods swing if they seem to want to. Don't hold rigidly to the 'neutral'. If any change or reaction occurs, just make a mental note of what happens, when and where; *don't* concern yourself for the moment with why or how it happened. Theorizing about real and apparent causes for the rods' movements at this stage will only be confusing and discouraging – so give yourself a chance, and don't!

So before you read any further, get up and do this *now*.

Well, how did it go? I imagine you were able to hold the rods fairly stable after a few minutes, but did anything else happen? If nothing else happened, don't worry about it, and certainly don't be discouraged. The balance between holding the rods stable but yet still allowing them to move is a subtle one – it does need practice, but it's no more difficult than, say, balancing the clutch and accelerator pedals when learning to drive a car. The trick here, as I mentioned earlier, is to *rest* your mind on the idea of keeping the rods stable – don't try too hard. If you can get that part sorted out, the rest, with a little practice, will follow.

Practice Just repeat that exercise from time to time in as many places as you can. Don't take it too seriously as yet. Treat your practice as a light-hearted game – a game with yourself rather than with others, for you may find that having people around you will tend (albeit often unconsciously) to be a discouragement rather than a help. Do be patient, give yourself a chance, and don't question everything as it happens – or doesn't happen! After all, your body has to learn a new skill, to learn what muscles to move when. Incidentally, don't practise too long at any one time, for you may find it surprisingly tiring at first, mentally if not physically.

If after quite a bit of practice the rods still only remain in 'neutral' and refuse to move 'of their own accord', there are three things to remember. First, check whether you're holding the rods in such a way that they can actually move! Secondly, remember to *relax*, both physically and mentally, and to allow the whole thing to 'work itself'. And third, practise at different places and different times, preferably alone, so that you have the maximum scope and the minimum interference.

Remember too that the idea of this practice is for you to learn the 'feel' of the rods. It's only the overall 'feel' that will tell you if the rods are just wobbling about or if they are moving 'of their own accord'. But learning *that* is all you should be doing or expecting at the moment – don't expect too much!

Interpretation and meaning

When you find that you can usually tell the difference between what seem to be 'true' and 'false' reactions – between those seemingly caused by something outside of you and those caused by yourself or by the wind catching the rods – move on to practical applications. In other words, this is the time to move on to *interpreting* the unlikely wigglings of your two pieces of bent wire.

Interpretation is finding the meaning of something that would otherwise be meaningless. And the rods' twitchings *are* of themselves meaningless: it's the interpretation, the meaning that you derive, that you *divine*, from those twitches that enables you to find water or whatever else it is that you're looking for. Hence water-*divining*, of course.

There are two kinds, or possibly two levels, of interpretation, one analytic and the other intuitive. The intuitive kind is based on inherent meaning, a sense of 'rightness' or 'wrongness' carried over by the reaction itself. It's somewhat too complex to explain further at this stage, and I'd rather leave it until later. But the analytic kind of interpretation is simpler, for it's based on repeatability: if a dowsing reaction is repeatable under the same conditions it is held to be 'true', and the meaning of that reaction is then derived from the conditions under which it took place. To give an example, one of these conditions is place or position: if a reaction repeatedly occurs at the same place, you can infer that something is *causing* the reactions at that place. And so on, other conditions of time, of number and other tests giving other meanings to the reactions. So by changing the conditions (done, among other things, by using different techniques) you can build up a picture of whatever it is you're looking for – its position, its size, its depth, its composition and qualities, in fact anything you need within the limits of analysis. But obviously it's best to start with something simple, and so to

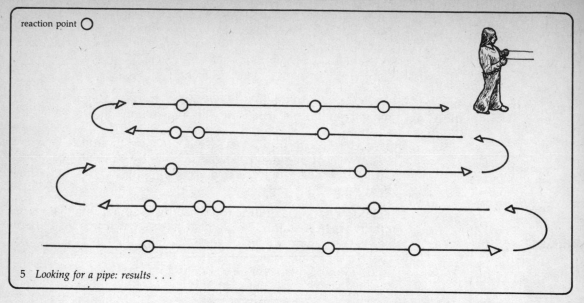

reaction point ○

5 *Looking for a pipe: results . . .*

apply the experience of the exercise you've already done I'd suggest that you start with basic water-divining: finding the branch water-main that leads into your house.

Position

Or, more precisely, finding the position of the pipe relative to the surface.

● Repeat the previous exercise of holding the rods in the neutral position while crossing and re-crossing the front of your house, or several houses. As before, don't question what happens, just let the rods 'work themselves'.

● Mark or mentally note any reaction points – a reaction point being the place directly beneath the rods at the time they react.

Your results, if you have been practising the first exercise, will probably look something like Fig. 5. But what does this mean? To use a radio analogy, some of these marks will be 'signal', or meaningful, and the remainder 'noise', or apparently meaning-

20

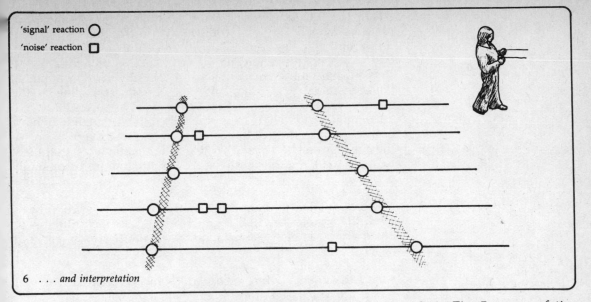

'signal' reaction ◯
'noise' reaction ☐

6 . . . and interpretation

less. But which ones? In the example in Fig. 5, some of the marks form clear zigzag lines, the marks being moved slightly away from a straight line in the direction the dowser was moving each time. Now one of these lines could well be a pipe, because while a zigzag pipe is most unlikely, many beginners react rather slowly, and thus tend to overshoot the 'true' reaction point – a sort of 'bracketing' effect. So let us consider the two clear zigzag lines as 'signals', and leave the rest, for the moment, as 'noise' (Fig. 6).

Do this exercise several times, and then compare the results to see if there is a repeatability of reaction at the same place. But *don't* go out expecting the same results each time, because among other things you might have been mistaken the first time, or else the lines may only have been 'noise' after all. Some things in dowsing have a nasty habit of not being what they seem – so beware! And so each time you do this exercise – or any dowsing exercise, for that matter – think of it and treat it as the first time every time.

Depth   Assuming that the lines in Fig. 6 which possibly imply water pipes *are* 'signal', the next problem is to find how deep they are. If the thing 'causing' the apparent line is only a few feet deep, then it probably is a pipe – a water pipe being the most likely, since most beginners react to water, especially moving water, to the almost total exclusion of anything else. But if the line gives a depth of tens of feet below the surface then whatever it is that's 'causing' it isn't likely to be a pipe – the old workmen may have been crazy, but they didn't often lay pipes *that* deep. Even so, the line may still be 'caused' by water, for 'water lines' that seem to imply small underground fissures or streams are surprisingly common.

There are plenty of depthing methods to choose from, but I think the simplest for the moment is the 'Bishop's Rule' – so called after a French bishop who *wasn't* the first to use it, but never mind.

● Find the line as before. Stop and stand directly above what appears to be its centre.

● Stop and relax completely for a moment, preferably putting your hands down to your sides – this is to conclude the first part, the location part, and to prepare for the next step. Now lift the rods back up into the working position and walk, very slowly, away from the centre of the line. Keep in mind that you're looking for the depth of the line.

● At some distance out the rods should react, possibly opening out instead of crossing over. Note that if this is working properly you should not be getting reactions in the same places as in the location part of the exercise.

● Do this several times, starting from the same point each time, but walking away in different directions.

These new reaction points should form an approximate circle centred on your starting point. The idea of the Bishop's Rule is that 'the distance out is the same as the distance down' – the

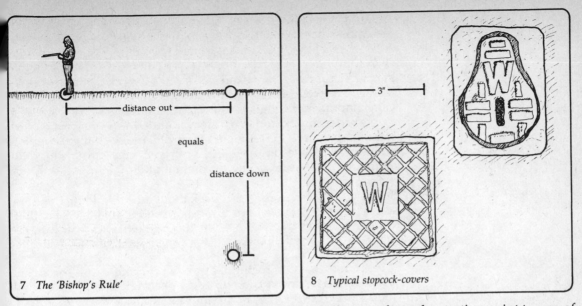

7 The 'Bishop's Rule'

8 Typical stopcock-covers

radius of the circle, the distance from the starting point to any of the new reaction points, is (or should be!) the same as the depth of the line, give or take a few per cent. Each of your new reaction points is a check on the others, and a check against being misled by other 'water lines': remember that it's always useful to check your results if you can.

So if this exercise implies that the 'pipe' is only a few feet below the surface, you can be fairly certain that it is the house main, or something like it – especially if on following its course you find that the line of the 'pipe' coincides with the stopcock cover just inside or outside the fence. To trace the course of the 'pipe', cross and recross the suspected line, as in the position part of the exercise, to build up a line of reaction-points implying the line of the 'pipe'. There are other ways of doing this, of course, but I'd prefer to leave them till later.

I've no doubt that you'll find these exercises invaluable if you now find that your water main has sprung a leak and you don't know where the external stopcock is – but otherwise do remember that the idea at the moment is simply to gain some experience of the 'feel' of dowsing, that's all.

Problems In describing these two exercises I've assumed that everything seems to be working all right. If it's not going all right, there are quite a number of things to check and variations to try – and it's a good idea to try some of the variations anyway. Problems come under three loose headings: problems with instruments, problems with the physical situation, and problems with what might be called approaches, or mental attitudes.

Problems with instruments Before you do anything else, check that you are holding the rods so that they can actually move, and can swing freely. Check that you are holding them as near to the horizontal as you can, so that they will react sharply to any hand movements.

If you feel that you're not happy with the angle rods, or if you just feel like having a change, try repeating the exercises with another instrument such as a pendulum or a spring rod. Both of these are described in the next chapter.

Physical problems An obvious problem is that there may be nothing there to find! Do try the exercises in a variety of places. I chose a water main for the example, but there are plenty of other kinds of moving water: for instance, you could look for conduits, soakaways and sewers in most areas, while in some cities there are canals and even rivers only a few feet underground.

Note that for the moment at least you will normally only be able to get the rods to react to *underground* water – not surface water – and for most people only to *moving* water at that. It's quite possible that you would get no reaction at all from the rods if you were to stand over the middle of an underground reservoir – though you ought to be able to get reactions from the inlet and outlet pipes. In the case of the water-main example in the exercise, you may find that it helps first to turn on a tap in the house for a couple of minutes, so as to get water flowing through the pipes.

In addition to the obvious problem of the wind catching the rods – a remedy here is to rest your thumbs lightly on the bends of the rods, to act as simple friction dampers – weather and similar changes in conditions can damp reactions right down to nothing at times. In my case I find it very difficult to work in hot muggy weather; for you it may be different, but find out for yourself. You'll probably find that the best weather for you will be that in which you feel most comfortable. But anyway it's best to repeat any exercise several times, and at different times of day.

The last physical problem for now is that of tiredness. If you find you are beginning to feel tired, physically or mentally, leave it till another day. If you don't, your results will almost certainly become erratic at best, and you'll just be discouraging yourself and wasting your time. Tied up with this is the fact that for many dowsers, especially beginners, dowsing can also be mentally very tiring, so limit your practice at the moment to short sessions of half an hour at most.

Problems with approaches   I'll be going into these in depth in Chapter 4, but briefly the main problem here is that your mental attitude has a critical effect – in both senses of the word – on the dowsing process. The catch is that a negative approach – 'it can't work, of course', or 'I suppose it'll never work for me' – or equally an overly positive approach – 'it *must* work for me', or 'trying' or 'concentrating' – will usually interfere with or neatly jam up the whole process. Dowsing seems to operate through a *receptive* state of mind, so don't be pessimistic, and don't try too hard. The key word here is 'rest': *rest* your mind on what you're doing. Just be a little patient; if you adopt a quiet confidence and just allow the rods to work themselves, the whole thing becomes much easier. But interfering interferes!

3 An assortment of instruments

Dowsing instruments are mechanical amplifiers of small neuromuscular reflexes, the most commonly used reflexes being those of the hands. In other words, they're things to tell you what your hands are doing. Most of them, like the angle rods I hope you *have* already been using, are very simple (the simpler the better, in my view), using basic mechanical principles to make small movements larger and more noticeable. In fact dowsing instruments can be divided into groups or classes according to the principle they use:

● angle rods use a *static neutral balance*

● the old hazel or whalebone 'spring rod', and most of the traditional tools like the bucket handle and the bow saw, are held in *unstable tension*

● the versatile 'pendulum' and its many variants use a *dynamic neutral balance*

and so on. These three types are the most commonly used, and so these are the ones I'll be using in my examples. Others, like the 'dial rod' or 'separation rod' and the willow or curtain-wire-loop (which use *changing separation of hands*) and the 'stick pad' of early radionic instruments (which uses *changing hand pressure*), are either awkward or rather limited in use, so I'd prefer to leave them out. If you do want to learn about them, they are described in other books on dowsing.

At the moment I'm experimenting with a range of electronic

amplifiers that could be used for dowsing – a galvanic skin response meter, which measures reflex changes of skin resistance; an electromyograph, which can measure the nervous impulses driving the muscles used in dowsing; and an electroencephalograph, used in this case to measure the changes in brain-wave-patterns coincident with the usual dowsing reactions. I'm working on them more out of interest than in the hope of developing them as viable dowsing instruments – but they may turn out to be more valuable than I expect, for some of the reflexes normally used in dowsing are not exactly famous for their speed and reliability, as you may have found already when doing the exercises.

Angle rods   I've already described how to make a pair of rods from coat hangers, how to hold them in use, and their basic reactions of crossing over, opening out, and swinging parallel to point out a direction, so I think all I need do here is describe adjustments for and of sensitivity, and some of the variations on the theme of angle rods.

Adjustments   Some of the adjustments you should already know, namely varying the angle of tilt from the horizontal to vary the delicacy of balance of the rods, and varying the amount of friction on their short arms – by grip or by thumb pressure – to counteract the effects of wind.

You can also vary the mechanical sensitivity and wind resistance of the rods by changing their lengths – which is easiest done by making a number of pairs of rods of different lengths. For angle rods I usually use eighth-inch welding or brazing rod: this is cheap, and comes in thirty-inch lengths. Allowing five inches for the short arm limits me to a maximum length of twenty-five inches for the long arm. At this length they are rather heavy, in that their weight tends to pull the wrists down – and they can also be a little dangerous to bystanders – but they have a great advantage in that they tend to remain stable, with a clear and positive reaction when they do react. At the other end of the scale a pair of rods only a few inches long will be very light, but they will also be over-sensitive to small hand movements.

The reason for this is that the longer the rod the greater its mass, and also the further away its centre of mass from the pivot point, both of these increasing its inertia. I think that because of the more obvious reaction a beginner is better off with a long pair of rods than a short one. For me the best compromise with eighth-inch rod is a length of about eighteen inches – which fortunately happens to be about the length of the base of a coat-hanger.

Another way of increasing the rods' inertia while still keeping them short is to add some weight to the tips of the rods. The lead wrapper from the top of a wine bottle will do nicely for this – find the right weight by trial and error. Alternatively you can use a heavier or thicker material for the rods; and conversely a lighter or thinner material will reduce the rods' inertia, but then they will be more seriously affected by the wind. Experiment to find out what suits you.

Variations Bearing in mind what I've just said about weight and so on, you can use any material you like – wood, metal or plastic – as long as the *mechanical* requirements of the rods are met. And while in theory the material you use *can* affect the dowsing process – more about this later – it seems that it will only do so if you want it to: so for the moment it's best to assume that in practice it doesn't matter what you use.

With regard to the use or non-use of sleeves, that again is a matter of personal choice. Some people prefer to do without them because they like to feel any reaction direct; others prefer to use sleeves because the rods swing rather more freely with them than without. But while I prefer to use simple wooden or metal sleeves myself, and would recommend you at least to try them yourself, I do feel that mounting everything in ball bearings – as the makers of the industrial 'Revealer' rods do – is needlessly expensive and complicated. And apart from that, ball-bearing rods have a heavy and awkward feel (in my experience at least) – using them is like trying to turn a gyroscope the wrong way. But if you want to use sleeves you can make them from any material, given the same limitations as for the rods

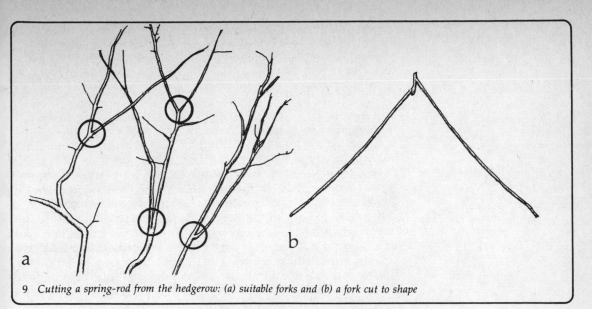

9 *Cutting a spring-rod from the hedgerow: (a) suitable forks and (b) a fork cut to shape*

themselves; in fact these limitations hold true for all dowsing instruments.

Spring rod This is usually a Y-shaped rod, sometimes made from a twig cut out of the hedgerow, sometimes made of two strips of springy material fastened together, and held in such a way that a small movement of the hands will make it spring sharply up or down.

Making If you're going to make a wooden one, look for a Y-shaped fork of any springy and resilient wood – hazel, hawthorn, cherry or dogwood, among others – with arms up to eighteen inches long, and between an eighth and a quarter inch thick. Cut it as shown in Fig. 9, being careful not to damage the tree or bush any more than you can help. Strip off any odd spikes or leaves, and the rod is ready for use. Note that as the twig dries out, it will become brittle, and snap; hawthorn dries out in a matter of hours, and even hazel may only last a few days. But rods made of metal, plastic or whalebone – the last is to my mind the best of the lot, but almost unobtainable nowadays – will last almost

29

indefinitely. For these take two strips of any springy, resilient material – again the length is a matter of personal choice, but eight to twelve inches should be fine for most materials – and tie, rivet or weld them together at one end, to make a Y-shape. Common sense should tell you to smooth any sharp edges!

Holding The idea is to hold it so that its natural springiness gives it a highly unstable balance. There are many ways of doing this, holding the rod at different heights and with the tip pointing away from you or towards you. Two grips are shown in Fig. 10, the first being suitable for a round-section twig, and the second for a rod of flat strip. In the first the arms of the twig go through loosely clenched fists, much as you did with the angle rods – only this time with the palms horizontal and facing up (as in the drawing), or horizontal and facing down. In the grip shown for the flat-strip rod the two strips are balanced on the first two fingers of each hand, with the thumbs applying some of the tension and also holding the strips against those fingers. The other two fingers of each hand should be folded in, more to keep them out of the way than anything else.

Using Once again, rest the mind on holding the rod in the neutral position, which, in both the examples given, is with the tip of the rod pointing horizontally away from you. Tense the rod and increase its springiness by twisting each arm into a curve: if you've got enough spring tension on the rod it will spring sharply up – or down – when you twist your wrists even slightly in a vertical plane. If you've got too little tension on the rod it will only move sluggishly, or not at all; if you've got too much tension you'll have one hell of a job holding the rod stable, especially when you're walking along: so there's another problem of balance here.

The rod's reactions are limited to neutral-to-up and neutral-to-down, and unlike the angle rods it won't return itself to neutral after a reaction – you have to stop and return it to neutral yourself by momentarily relaxing the tension on the rod. Whenever I use a long spring rod it always manages to hit me on the nose as it springs up – so watch out!

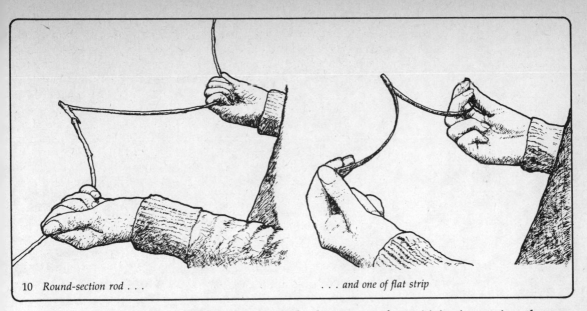

10 *Round-section rod . . .*   *. . . and one of flat strip*

Adjustments   The only practical adjustment of sensitivity is varying the tension with which you hold the rod. Generally speaking, the greater the tension – the degree to which the spring part of the rod is tensioned – the sharper will be the rod's reaction to small wrist-movements, simply because the greater the tension the greater the degree of instability of the rod. You can change the tension by twisting your wrists in a horizontal plane, or by bringing them nearer together or further apart, or both – Fig. 11 shows a slack rod and a tense rod.

The most common faults in using a spring rod are all to do with its tension – either changing the tension half-way through doing something, or holding the rod with too much tension, or with insufficient tension for it to react quickly. Incidentally, the 'bracket' or 'overshoot' effect I mentioned earlier tends to be worst with a spring rod for this reason. Another fault is holding the rod so tightly and with so much tension that either you tire quickly, or your muscles 'lock' to such an extent that the rod can't possibly move. Do remember to *relax* as much as possible,

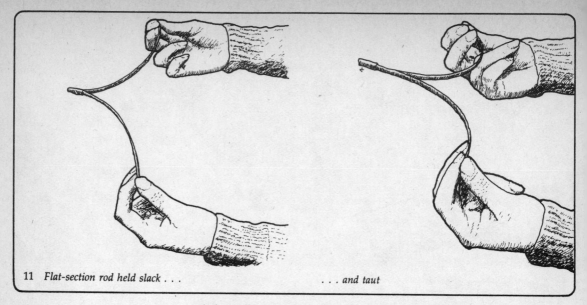

11 *Flat-section rod held slack . . .*   *. . . and taut*

while still applying enough tension to the rod. And, as usual, experiment to find a balance that suits you.

Variations Anything that can be held in unstable tension can be used as a spring rod, so variations on the general theme are legion. In addition to the more usual twigs and whalebone rods, one eighteenth-century book on dowsing lists as spring rods a bow saw, an open book, a pair of scissors, a clock spring, a pair of clay pipes, a metal ruler, a knife and fork, a bucket handle and even a twisted German sausage! So if you want to be different, use your ingenuity, but do remember that the sensitivity of the rod will depend on its springiness and resilience. In other words, be realistic!

Pendulum In dowsing usage a pendulum is 'any small weight connected to the hand by a flexible link', which usually means a plumb-bob hanging on the end of a piece of string. But when I say 'any small weight', I do mean that practically any small weight will do: in fact hunting for things that can be used for pendulums

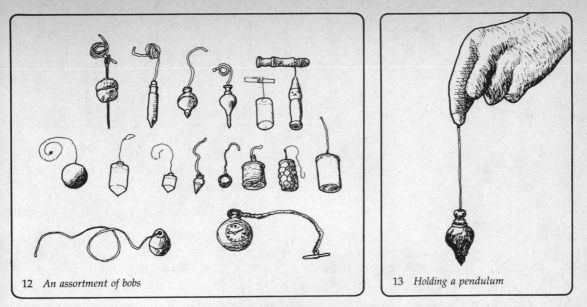

12 *An assortment of bobs*

13 *Holding a pendulum*

has become one of my crazier minor hobbies. The choice of a bob for a pendulum is more a matter of whimsy than anything else, though again do be realistic. Remember that from the mechanical point of view of inertia and balance, a bob should be at least somewhat symmetrical around its vertical axis, and shouldn't be too long on that axis, either, or else you will find that it will tend to wobble about rather than swing smoothly as you use it. The onion-shaped brass builder's plumb-bob fits the mechanical requirements perfectly – but since they're getting rare and expensive, I now search for them in every old ironmonger's shop that I can find! As for weight, start with something weighing about two ounces, hanging from about three inches of string – but more about this later, under 'Adjustments'.

Making   While you *can* make your own bob you'll probably need a lathe to do it, so it's generally easier to buy or find something to do the job instead. Tie it to a length of cord, string, fishing line, old bootlace or whatever, about a foot long. When you've done that, you have a pendulum!

33

Holding   After quite a bit of experimenting I feel that the grip shown in Fig. 13 is the most practical one, from the mechanical point of view at least. Hold the cord between the first finger and thumb (of either hand), leaving about three inches of cord between them and the bob. 'Lose' the remainder of the cord by wrapping it round your other fingers, or else its tag end is bound to get tangled up with the bob at the wrong moment. The thumb and forefinger thus fix the effective length of the bob-and-string pendulum, and you can easily adjust that length by small amounts by gripping the cord at different points, since most of the weight is actually carried by the cord wrapped round the other fingers. There are many other ways of holding this kind of pendulum, of course, but since most of them cause the effective length of the pendulum to 'wander' in use, I would recommend that you start with this one.

Using   You *can* use the-pendulum-at-rest as the neutral position, as some dowsers do, but I've always found this awkward. I prefer to use the-pendulum-in-oscillation as the neutral position,

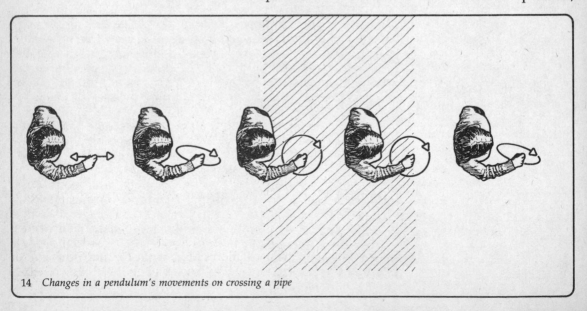

14   *Changes in a pendulum's movements on crossing a pipe*

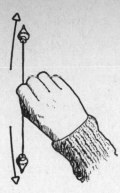

15 *'Neutral' seen from above*

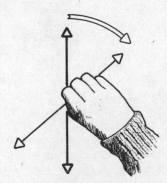

16 *Directional reaction of a pendulum*

Adjustments

which I feel helps the pendulum to move smoothly and quickly from neutral to reaction. So swing the pendulum lightly backwards and forwards; rest your mind on its oscillation so that its line of swing, its *axis* of swing, remains stable, as a line ahead. There are then two kinds of reaction: a change from oscillation to gyration, either clockwise or anti-clockwise, and a change in the axis of swing.

The first, the change from oscillation to gyration, is the usual reaction to an object – such as the water main in the exercises of the last chapter. If you rest your mind on keeping the oscillation stable, walking slowly, the pendulum's oscillation should change to gyration as you cross the pipe, and then return to oscillation once you have passed it. But if you walk too quickly, or if you use far too long a string (so that the bob takes a couple of seconds to swing back and forth each time), you'll have gone past the reaction-point before the pendulum has had time even to begin to change its movement – so watch out! It helps if you adjust the length of the cord so that the pendulum's rate of swing matches your pace – I usually try to make it do one swing to one pace. The pendulum may gyrate either way; and though the different directions of gyration can be made to mean different things, as I'll explain later, you'll probably find it easiest at the moment to use oscillation as neutral, and either gyration as reaction.

The other kind of reaction, the change of axis of swing, is a directional reaction, much like that of the angle rods turning parallel to point out a direction. You don't need this yet, but I will be describing its uses later.

There are two adjustments for sensitivity on a pendulum, namely changing its weight, and changing the length of its cord. The first of these is more a matter of practicality than sensitivity, I suppose: if you're going to be walking about you'll need a heavy bob – somewhere from two to five ounces – so that its inertia will keep the oscillation stable; while for map dowsing, or other finely detailed work, you'll need a light bob – down to half an ounce or so – that can react quickly to small changes in hand-movements. You can increase the weight of a bob by adding bits of lead, but it isn't all that easy to reduce it – it's simpler to collect a range of bobs. Mine range from a quarter-ounce to five ounces, in brass, steel, wood and plastic – though I admit I don't *need* that many. If you can only afford or find one pendulum bob, note that a heavy one is generally more useful than a light one, but I realize that it does rather depend on what you can get hold of.

The adjustment of the length of the cord is important – so much so that more than one writer has devoted a whole chapter to the subject. The optimum length of the cord is dependent on the weight of the bob and on what can only be called the natural frequency of the operator's hand. To take an analogy, that of knocking in a nail with a hammer: most people will knock in a nail by hitting it at short regular intervals, and this is somewhat analogous to the rate of swing of a pendulum. The frequency of hits with the hammer will depend partly on its weight, partly on the effective length of its handle, and partly on a number of body conditions like wrist strength and applied force and so on, all of these making up a natural resonance or frequency. So with a pendulum the first of these conditions is fairly obvious: the heavier the bob, the longer the time of swing needed, and thus the longer the length of cord needed. On average the length for a four-ounce bob will be around four or five inches, while for a half-ounce bob the length will be more like one to one-and-a-half inches. But this is what you might call the coarse adjustment of the pendulum: you then need to adjust the length of the cord finely to match the rate of swing with the natural resonance, the natural movement of your hand. Raise or lower the bob a little until it feels right.

If the adjustment is very much out you'll notice – especially with a heavy bob – that the pendulum's oscillation is jerky and clumsy, while if the adjustment is 'dead on' the oscillation will be smooth and seemingly effortless. The pendulum will also be more reliable as an instrument if it's properly adjusted, but fortunately it isn't all that critical in the early stages. Getting the adjustment right for you is just a matter of practice, and after a while you should find that you can pick up any pendulum and automatically hold it at the right length.

Variations   Most pendulums are bobs suspended on a piece of string (or something like it), but from time to time I come across one that has a bob mounted on a spring instead. Another one I have used consisted of a long springy rod – a standard welding rod, in fact – with one end set in a handle. Both of these work in the same way as an ordinary pendulum, and need to be adjusted in the same way for the same reasons. Both have the advantage that they can be used at any angle – they're usually used pointing in front of the operator, unlike the ordinary pendulum, which must be used hanging down; both have the disadvantage that they are difficult to use for directional work.

Which instrument is best?   All of them! They all have their uses, their advantages and disadvantages. The pendulum is the most versatile of the three, partly because of its range of reactions, partly because one hand is left free to do anything else that's needed; while the spring rod is the least versatile and most tiring to use. But the pendulum is the most susceptible of the three to psychological interference (the subject of the next chapter); while in foul and windy weather there is nothing to beat the positive all-or-nothing reaction of a spring rod! So it's not so much a case of which tool is better, but more one of choosing the right tool for the job.

Body reactions   The instruments I've described are tools to tell you what your hands are doing, and not much more. But you can use other reflexes besides those used to move these instruments, and in time you may notice that your body reacts in other ways, simultaneously with moving your instruments, as you pass over the reaction-points that they show. Several dowsers have found that a tingling sensation in their hands coincident with the instrument's reaction has turned out to be more reliable than the instrument itself, and now dowse with their bare hands held in front of them, as though playing blind-man's buff without the blindfold.

There are many other 'body reactions' you can use: a momentary stomach ache or feeling of loss of balance; a tightening of the back or neck muscles; a tic of the eyelids; a yawn; even, as happens to one friend, a sequence of hiccups. While most if not all people can train themselves to use the hand reflexes, different people have different natural body reactions, so learn to notice how *your* body as a whole reacts during dowsing operations. If you can learn to use your body as a dowsing tool you can do away with the crutch-like instruments I've described – for in reality they're only crutches for your intuition. One of the most important things you can learn in dowsing is that the aim is not – as it is in the more conventional sciences – to build ever bigger and more complicated crutches, but rather to move towards absolute simplicity. And what could be simpler than using yourself?

Causes and effects in dowsing

All of this brings me back to what I said at the beginning of this chapter: 'Dowsing instruments are mechanical amplifiers of small neuromuscular reflexes, the most commonly used reflexes being those of the hands.' The point of this seemingly pompous statement is that in almost all cases the cause of the instrument's moving is a neuromuscular reflex, a joint reflex between a part of the nervous system and the muscles connected up with it. Now that's easy enough to demonstrate; but if you want to find the cause of a dowsing reaction past that point, you're going to get into an awful mess, which is why I don't like theorizing about possible ultimate causes of dowsing reactions.

The reason is that there are two kinds of reflexes involved: the first are the simple automatic reflexes, like the one below the knee that a doctor tests with his hammer, and the second is a very un-simple collection of mental reflexes, such as conditioned reflexes; and it's usually impossible to tell which kind is involved at any one time. Ordinary things such as heat and sounds and smells, and even small changes in background radiation and local magnetic or gravitational fields, can and do trigger off the simple reflexes; but the triggers for the mental reflexes are extremely complex, by definition not necessarily physical, and quite possibly infinite and indeterminate. But the very fact of their complexity, and the other fact that they are tied up with the mind anyway, leads us on to that horrible problem of psychophysiological – or 'psychological' – interference in the dowsing process. So on to the next chapter!

4 Psychological interference

Don't skip this chapter – it's important!

Psychological interference is a general term covering a range of problems, all of which involve the intrusion of the mind into the dowsing process. This intrusion, however, is a two-edged sword, for while it is true that it is the cause of most mistakes in dowsing, it is also the key to its surprising flexibility as a subject and a tool. Dowsing is essentially subjective and personal, and to produce reliable results this subjectivity needs to be carefully watched and controlled. But what are the key factors in this subjectivity, and how can they be controlled?

There are three major points that need to be closely watched. The first of these is attempting to control consciously the automatic part of the dowsing process; the second is the intrusion of conscious and semiconscious assumptions and prejudices, and the related problem of failing to keep your mind on what you're supposed to be doing; and the third is the intrusion of unconscious assumptions and prejudices. The last of these is by far the most serious. There are other problems, of course, but they seem to be relatively minor, and should sort themselves out with practice and experience.

Meddling and muddling Otherwise known as attempting to interfere with the automatic part of the dowsing process, the first of these three problems. In any skill you have to practise until the movements and actions of the manual part of the skill become automatic, become a sequence of reflex actions and reactions. Once it knows what to do, the body can get on with the job quickly and efficiently – as long as the mind doesn't confuse the issue with contradictory orders. It's rather like riding a pushbike: in order to ride you must balance, balancing a number of opposing forces, without really knowing how or why; and if you do start to think or worry about balancing, you promptly fall off! The same happens with a nervous tic, where the only result of trying to control the tic is to make it worse; and the same is true of dowsing, where I've seen several would-be dowsers shatter their hazel twigs by trying to stop them turning in their hands. With a little practice, the reflex reaction patterns for any given instrument will establish themselves quite quickly; and once this has happened, leave them alone. Don't meddle!

Direction and redirection

But you do need to control your instruments: you do need to direct the kind of movements they make, so as to produce different types of reactions for different problems; and so you do need to control these reactions in some way. You can't do this directly – so you have to do it indirectly. On a pushbike you think about which way you want to turn rather than thinking about how to steer the bike, and in dowsing it's best to redirect your conscious attention on to the effect – or intended effect – of a given reflex movement, so as to let the body produce, unconsciously, the right reflex or series of reflexes. Watch the effect, listen to the effect, and your body will produce the right 'cause'. The simplest way of doing this in practice is to treat the instrument as if it has a life and mind of its own – which in most senses it hasn't, but that's beside the point. I sometimes think of instruments as being like cantankerous children: they won't work unless you ask them to, and certainly won't work if you try and force them to; they occasionally lie, and sometimes sulk and refuse to work at all; so you have to use a little guile, a little ingenuity and a little wit to get the results you need.

As an illustration of this, here is another experiment. I've designed it for a pendulum or a pendulum-based instrument; you can use other types, but they're rather impractical for this.

● Take a pendulum and hold it in neutral – in other words, in oscillation. Check that the adjustment is at least approximately right – this is important.

- Tell the pendulum to gyrate clockwise (anti-clockwise if you prefer, but do be specific, or else it – in other words, your reactions – may get confused). The pendulum's movement should change from oscillation to at least a semblance of gyration in the specified direction within a few seconds.

- Now tell it to stop. It should now either return to neutral, or else come to a complete standstill. If it does come to a standstill, start it swinging in neutral again.

- Now do this again, but this time don't order the pendulum to move, just *think* of it moving from oscillation to gyration, build up in your mind an image of it doing so. And bring it back to neutral in the same way.

This last part, incidentally, can also be used as a test of the pendulum's adjustment. If the adjustment is right, you should still be able to do it blindfold; if it's not right, you won't be able to do so.

Casual intrusions Or, the intrusion of conscious and semi-conscious prejudices and assumptions into the dowsing process. These prejudices and assumptions breed a collection of thoughtless and thoughtful blunders, of which the worst is jumping to conclusions. So, to demonstrate this, another experiment:

- Mark a line on the ground – anywhere will do. Mark it with chalk or a piece of string, or something equally visible.

- Now take any instrument, hold it in the working position, and walk towards the line. Casually but convincingly inform yourself that the line you've drawn denotes an underground stream. Note what happens as you cross the line.

- Rub out or remove the line, and do the same thing again. Inform yourself – convincingly! – that there is a stream below the point where the line was. And again see if any reaction occurs.

- Now, to invert the whole experiment, go outdoors to some place where you have repeatedly had reactions before with your instruments. Go over the place as you have done before, but this time inform yourself that there is nothing there to be found, or that dowsing is all nonsense anyway. Is there any change from your usual reaction?

The point I'm trying to make here is that you have to watch out for simple slips like 'I got a reaction there last time so I should get one there now'. You probably will get another reaction there now – but that doesn't mean to say that it's right. Things do change, and equally you may have been misled the first time anyway. For the same reason beware of allowing the assumptions and controls for one part of an experiment to run on into the next, or you will get into exactly the same kind of mess. Always pause for a moment and clear your mind of the mental furniture you used for the last part of an exercise before repeating it or starting a new one.

Be observant, by all means, but don't let that careful observation of the things around you trick you into making casual assumptions, or into jumping to 'obvious' conclusions. You have to watch yourself, and your thoughts in general, as well as your surroundings.

Deliberate intrusions This is the other side of that two-edged sword, the useful side: it's simply the deliberate application of what would otherwise be casual intrusion as a method of selecting or filtering out different bits of information – sorting out a 'signal' from the background 'noise', in the radio analogy. Like weeds, casual intrusion is only a nuisance in the wrong place and at the wrong time!

The simplest application of this is to damp down a reaction that is too powerful, or to cut out the reaction to a powerful stream so as to trace a weaker one – the equivalent of the volume and squelch controls on a radio. This is done, as in the experiments on page 41, by thinking 'with intent' of what you want done: I usually do it by saying to myself 'All right, I know *that's* there; now what else is there?' – I hope that's self-explanatory.

The most useful application of these deliberate intrusions is qualitative, as the equivalent of the tuner controls on a radio. To explain, when you started on the experiments at the beginning of this book, it didn't much matter what you were 'picking up' – anything would do, to give you some kind of experience. But obviously as you start on serious and practical work you'll need to know what it is that you're reacting to, and preferably only to react to what you're looking for. One of the ways of doing this – there are others – is to apply this deliberate intrusion, in that by stating what it is that you're looking for, you can effectively cut out reactions to anything else. You'll need to state what you're looking for with care and precision, in the same way that if you mistune a radio you'll get interference creeping in. But the great advantage of this technique is that it is extremely simple, for as one friend describes it:

'If I'm looking for something I have to have in my mind an image of that object that I'm looking for, either a mental or perhaps a verbal image, and unless I've got that loosely in my mind one doesn't find these things. If you're walking along looking for water and you're thinking about, oh, a train which might be passing by, well, your thoughts wander, and you don't get the reaction. You've got to have your mind pinpointed and focused on the object that you're looking for.'

So watch out for those low-flying trains . . . of thought! But anyway, more about this mental selection or 'tuning' in the next few chapters.

Unconscious intrusions These interfere in the same way as casual intrusions, but their effect on the results is often more serious simply because they *are* unconscious. Some of the limits and prejudices which can foul up the whole process with 'instant doubt' and wild assumptions (especially in the more complex areas like map dowsing) are so deep-seated even in those who are honestly trying to be open-minded, that reliable results can be very hard to come by. In theory the only way of handling this problem is to *isolate the self entirely* from the process, with the sole exception of that part of the self that is applying whatever conscious directions and controls are needed – 'the observer, in observing, must play no part in the observation'.

This is a theoretical ideal, of course, but in practice and with experience you should be able to come pretty close to it. I think that the problem of isolating the self from the process has to be tackled in a contemplative or meditative way (in the open rather than the specifically religious sense of the words) in some form of reflection on yourself and the work being done. If you're already experienced in some form of meditation, simply apply it while you're working, either direct or with suitable modifications. If not, try resting your mind on three points: on the balance of the instrument; on where you are; and on the problem-at-hand, the particular part of the technique that you're doing at that time. And I do mean *rest* the mind – rest the mind on that 'tripod'. Apart from that part of the conscious mind that is directing the operation – framing the problem-at-hand, framing 'the image of the object that you're looking for' – the mind must be involved *receptively*, not actively.

So 'trying to get a result' is out; 'concentrating' in the usual sense is out – and so is doubting your ability to do it, for that's an active state of mind too! Looking for proof, trying to 'prove' something, is also a form of doubt, and so that has to go by the board as well – although it will work well enough if you let it, you won't be able to 'prove beyond reasonable doubt' that dowsing works, to anyone who decides they aren't going to believe you.

While you do need to be watching yourself and your thoughts, that watching should always be quiet and unobtrusive: if your watching becomes so intense that you question every move you make, you'll grind to a halt in a confusion of self-doubt – and that won't help you to be confident either. So treat the whole thing fairly light-heartedly. Don't be *too* serious!

Summary

- To avoid getting in a tangle over handling an instrument, redirect your attention away from your hands onto the instrument itself. Just allow it to 'work itself' – don't meddle!

- Watch your thoughts – don't get tricked into jumping to 'obvious' conclusions. And keep your mind on the job!

- Stop and clear your mind of the mental furniture of the last step of any experiment before going on to the next. Always try to do each step as though you've never done it before – this is particularly important if you're repeating an earlier experiment. Just relax, both physically and mentally, and see what happens.

- Build a mental balance round your position, the instrument and the problem at hand. You need to be mentally relaxed so that the various intrusions can be controlled, but yet alert enough to watch for the intrusions and for the instrument's reactions; you need *mentally* to hold the instrument stable but yet be able to react to any 'outside' change.

- The two kinds of balance, the mental and the physical, are the keys to reliable results: if either or both of them go wrong, so will the results. This shouldn't matter too much with the kind of experiments I've described so far, but in some areas such as medical dowsing a bad mistake could possibly be fatal. It's all too easy to fool yourself – so beware!

This balancing act isn't as difficult as it sounds. Assuming that you will actually allow yourself to relax, both in body and in mind, it should sort itself out and become automatic with practice and experience. *Don't* worry about it, and *don't* try to force it along – for, as with learning to ride a pushbike, worrying if you'll *ever* learn to balance the thing will only be a hindrance to its becoming automatic. So you don't even need to think about it: just bear the various guidelines in mind while you're working, that's all.

Practice again We've now reached the end of this practical introduction. Before you go on to look at some other dowsing techniques, I would suggest that you do a little more practice on the exercises I've described so far. Keep the guidelines above, and those of Chapter 2, in mind while you're doing so; if you do, you should find that your results will become steadily more reliable. Remember, though, that unless you're going to use your experience of those exercises to find a lost drain or a leak in a water pipe, precise and reliable results aren't all that important at the moment, but the practical experience is, for it's only through that experience that dowsing becomes meaningful.

PART TWO

Techniques

5 Introduction to techniques

Dowsing is rather like the old game of 'Twenty questions': you ask Nature a series of questions, to which she (through your instruments) will only answer 'Yes' or 'No'. You can also coax a direction to a place out of her, and sometimes a proportion or number; sometimes you can even get her to tell you when your questions are leading you off down a blind alley; but that's the lot. Nature plays hard to get.

So you have to frame your questions, to set up conditions within them, in such a way that one of these answers will actually be meaningful and tell you what you want to know. There are a number of basic types of question in dowsing, a number of basic *techniques*, which are common to all its applications – hence the reason why I'm dealing with techniques here, rather than as individual techniques used for specific applications. If I tried to describe every possible question and technique that you could use to tackle every possible dowsing problem, I'd have to fill volume after volume – and you'd never use most of them anyway. But if I reduce the range of questions down to their basic types, you should be able to see how to adapt these basic questions, these basic techniques, to tackle any problem you need.

To give an example, let's say that you've been asked by a cattle farmer to find a new water supply sufficient for the needs of his cattle. This overall problem consists of a number of subsidiary problems – for instance, you need to find:

● The *presence* of water (a qualitative problem).

- The *quality* of that water: its potability, mineral content and so on (also a qualitative problem).

- Its *position* relative to the surface (positional).

- Its *course* and *direction of flow* (positional and directional).

- Its *depth* relative to the surface (positional and/or quantitative).

- The *amount or volume* of water available (quantitative).

and so on. But you can see how these apparently very different problems are falling into three categories of qualitative problems, quantitative problems and problems of both position and direction to a position – and you'll see, in the next three chapters, how the basic techniques for each of these categories, and the ideas behind them, can be adapted to suit any problem you need.

As you read through my descriptions of the various techniques, you may (if you've read other books on dowsing) notice that a number of traditional techniques – 'solar ray', 'fundamental ray', 'series', 'serial number' and others – are either missing, or else only fleetingly mentioned. This is intentional: for from my own experience of learning dowsing, and of helping others to learn, I've found that their excessive complexity serves only to get beginners utterly confused. They may be more useful for experienced dowsers, but then this book isn't really for them anyway. Myself, I prefer to keep things as simple as possible.

There is a further category of positional techniques which, while not radically different from the earlier category, do allow you greatly to extend the range and scope of dowsing. These positional techniques – map dowsing, time dowsing and so on – allow you to operate in different places and different times from the one your body is in; these are best described as positional techniques in non-normal space-time, and are discussed in Chapter 9. With them you can work from a map, for instance, to find the most likely areas for water before you go to that cattle farm; with them you can work from a series of points in time to find out how much the amount of water available varies throughout the year. But they are by definition mental techniques rather than physical ones, and therefore need much stricter control of the mind in using them than the more conventional positional and directional techniques – hence the separate category.

So I've split the techniques into these four categories – qualitative, positional and directional, quantitative, and positional in non-normal space-time – with each of these categories forming one of the next four chapters. This part of the book is meant to be more of a reference section than anything else, but since in most cases I've shown them as I would use them for water-divining, please note that:

● The techniques as shown may (and probably will) need to be modified and adapted to suit other applications.

● The techniques are shown and described for angle rods, spring rod and pendulum, and then only for those instruments I have found it practical to use for each. You may need to modify some techniques to suit any other instrument you may be using.

● The techniques and instruments are described and shown in the way I would normally use them. They may or may not work in the same way for you, so it's important to experiment and check for yourself.

Between them and with suitable linking and/or adaptation, these techniques should be able to tackle almost any dowsing problem. But the rest is up to you: much of your skill in dowsing will depend on your ability and ingenuity in breaking problems down to a form that can be handled by your instruments -- and that means inventing new techniques as you go along. So use this techniques section not as a textbook of 'objective facts', but as a source of ideas from which to develop your own style and your own techniques.

6 Qualities

Samples   The main traditional technique is one of using samples of the object you want to find. The idea is derived largely from the concept of 'sympathy': to find an object you have to have something similar to it or of it that will be 'sympathetic' to the object. So a sample for any given object is something that has one or more shared properties or qualities with that object, the usual shared property being that both are made of the same material. To give a couple of examples, a sample for a lost brass button would be some other brass object, while a sample for oil would be a little bottle of oil, or a range of little bottles containing different types and qualities of oil. A sample for a particular quality of, say, mineral water would be bottled in the same way as for oil, but traditionally in most water divining no sample is used, because the sample for water in general is the water in your body.

But there are other properties which can be shared. In using a coin as a sample to find another coin, the shared properties include not only material but also the individual components of the alloy, the coin's shape and size and possibly weight, and so on – you might include age and function as well. So in theory you could use any disc-shaped object as a sample for a lost coin, but then you might well turn up other disc-shaped objects (such as washers and buttons) instead.

Samples of and for people are, interestingly, the same as in medieval witchcraft and sorcery: organic samples such as hair, nail parings, a blood-spot on a bit of paper, or a urine sample; a signature or a sample of handwriting; a handkerchief or a frag-

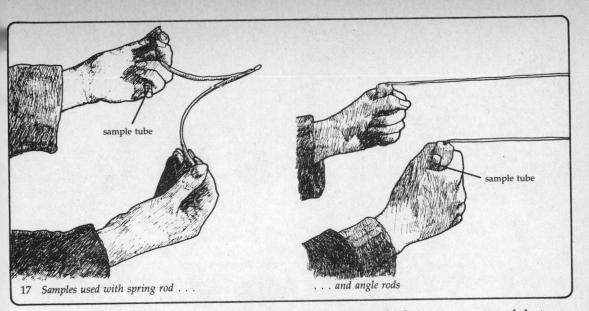

17 *Samples used with spring rod . . .*   *. . . and angle rods*

sample tube

sample tube

ment of clothing; or anything which is or was part of that person, or else belongs or belonged to them. Incidentally, some writers say that an envelope, for instance, is useless as a sample of the writer of the letter because other people have handled it in the meantime. I haven't found this necessarily to be the case, but you'll have to find out for yourself: a lot of this depends on what you believe or expect. In addition to the more physical samples, images such as photographs, drawings or – I suppose – wax models can also be used, the limit being whether the image is meaningful and recognizable (to the dowser at least) as an image of the required person. The fact that all these bits and pieces can be used successfully, in what I suppose can only be called a magical operation, means that we ought to treat the sorcery beliefs and the fear of photography of some primitive and not-so-primitive peoples with a rather more healthy respect.

Using samples If you're using angle rods or a spring rod the sample should be held – preferably touching the instrument, though I don't really

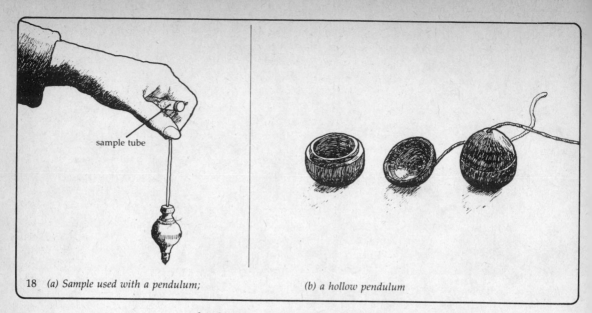

sample tube

18 *(a) Sample used with a pendulum;*   *(b) a hollow pendulum*

think it's essential. Liquid samples such as oil or water have to be put into bottles, of course. If you're using a pendulum, you can hold the sample in either the pendulum hand or free hand, or else you can make or find a suitable hollow bob that has a space inside for the sample. Remember that it will need a close-fitting lid if you're going to put liquids inside it.

The instrument should react directly above the object, or any object for which your sample will act as a sample. This reaction-only-above-the-object is rather limiting, and for most work I'd recommend you to use some other positional or directional technique – for which see Chapter 8. Incidentally, according to tradition the instrument must be made of insulating material, such as wood or plastics, or have any metal parts insulated from the hands. This is supposed to prevent the material of the instrument accidentally becoming the operating sample. Conversely, tradition says, you can use the material of the instrument as a sample if you want to, so for example if you want to find brass, use a brass pendulum.

The idea of the sample is that the instrument should react only to those things that are 'sympathetic' to the sample. The trouble is that you're likely to turn up other things as well as or, sadly, instead of the object that you're looking for: for instance, if your sample is a copper coin, you may turn up bits of copper pipe, old brass hinges and the knob off the end of an old bedstead, as well as the coins you're after. This lack of precision is the main problem with the traditional sample techniques.

Inherent problems in using samples

Taking the example of a copper coin a little further, you'll probably find that not only will the sample pick out anything that has even a trace of copper or one of its compounds in it, but that it will also start collecting along the lines of all the other properties of the sample – shape, size, weight, and so on. And while it's doing this, it will probably miss the coin you're looking for, despite the sample and the object sharing many properties while some of your other finds may share only one. But the sample is supposed to be a sort of resonant filter which not only reacts to similar objects but also screens out any other influences. So where is it going wrong? The problem seems to be a dilemma tied up with the original source of this idea of 'sympathy', the Platonic concept of the 'Same' and the 'Different' within the same object: for in using a sample are you dealing with a sympathy or harmony of Samenesses, or a discord of Differences? The instruments won't say.

'Rates' and 'series'

Before leaving this concept of resonance or sympathy, I ought to mention two other techniques with much the same limitations but which use that concept rather differently.

The late Tom Lethbridge was the chief exponent of the 'long pendulum' technique, in which the resonance between the object and the dowser is achieved by using specific lengths of cord on a pendulum. Different objects resonate with the pendulum at different lengths of cord, the length of the cord being called the 'rate' for that object since it gives the pendulum a specific rate of swing.

It's often used in conjunction with the series technique, or the

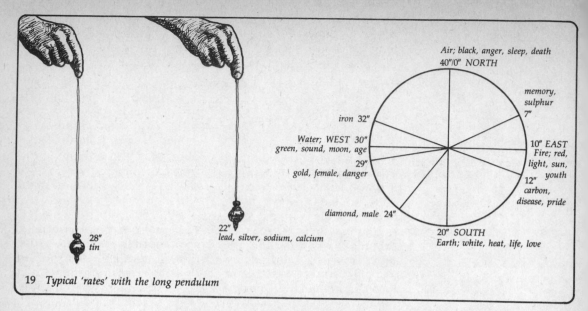

Air; black, anger, sleep, death
40"/0" NORTH

memory,
sulphur
7"

iron 32"

Water; WEST 30"
green, sound, moon, age

29"
gold, female, danger

10" EAST
Fire; red,
light, sun,
youth

12"
carbon,
disease, pride

diamond, male 24"

20" SOUTH
Earth; white, heat, life, love

28"
tin

22"
lead, silver, sodium, calcium

19   *Typical 'rates' with the long pendulum*

closely related one of serial number. The series of an object is the number of gyrations a pendulum will make over an object before returning to oscillation; and the serial number is the number of times the pendulum can be made to move from oscillation to gyration on re-crossing the object until the pendulum becomes 'saturated' and refuses to move to gyration. Sometimes series is called serial number, and vice-versa, by the way, which nicely confuses the issue! According to one dowser the series and serial number for copper are five and seven respectively. In theory every object is supposed to have a different combination of series and serial number – and fundamental ray, solar ray, polar meridian, rate, wavelength and all manner of other semi-physical attributes.

But the trouble is that these systems are even more complicated than that, for sometimes different objects *do* have the same rates and series and everything else – and also the different numbers and other attributes seem to be different for almost every dowser, so if you want to use these attributes you'll have to build up your own system. And that can take a long time. Besides, you should already know how clumsy and slow a foot-long pendulum can be, so do you fancy trying to use a *three*-foot long one, as the Lethbridge system sometimes demands?

I haven't the space to go into these in any more detail, but if you do want to use them they are described fully in Leth-bridge's, de France's and Mermet's books, which are listed in the Appendix on page 154.

Mental qualitative techniques

There are two groups of mental techniques, the first being a mental version of the samples techniques, and the second being a system of mental questions sometimes known as the 'Yes'/'No' system.

The mental-samples group of techniques have two great advantages over the physical samples techniques. Firstly, since they are ideas or images held in the mind rather than objects held in the hand, the system as a whole is far more flexible: for as well as physical samples it includes verbal images, visualiza-tions and a great string of different kinds of symbolic images – colour, sound, pattern and so on. Secondly, by *stating in your mind the context in which you are using the sample*, you can override the inherent problem of the imprecision of the physical samples system. These mental samples work as a form of the deliberate intrusion described in the last chapter, so the reliability is dependent on the clarity with which you frame the sample or image in your mind, and the degree of care with which you hold it there while working. Gently does it!

So now a brief survey of the different kinds of mental samples.

Physical samples

. . . are used in exactly the same way as in traditional dowsing, except that your mental approach to the problem should be rather different. So two points: firstly, use the sample as an *aide-memoire*, something on which to rest your attention, rather than as some physical or semi-physical 'resonator'; and second-ly, remember to frame the context in which you're using the sample. To use my earlier example, the context in which you use a copper coin as a sample could be as a sample for copper, for objects containing copper compounds, for coins, for specifically copper coins, for disc-shaped objects in general, and so on. So which context are you using? Keep that context in mind as well as the image of the sample.

Verbal images . . . are basically the same as above, but now you discard the sample itself and use a verbal statement of the problem instead. For example, the problem above becomes 'I'm looking for copper coins'. There's no need to state it out loud, of course – it's not supposed to be a magical spell, a statement of magical 'words of power'! It's just a statement of intent in your mind, something on which to rest your attention.

Visualization . . . or, literally, imagination. Your ability to use this will depend on your ability to visualize or build up a picture in your mind of the object that you're looking for – it's basically the same as the verbal image, but use and construct a visual image instead. You can always use a verbal statement along with it, of course. If you assemble the image with care and hold it clearly in your mind, this is probably the most precise and reliable of all the mental qualitative techniques.

Symbols and symbolic images As I said earlier, there's quite a string of these. The technique is the same as with the other kinds of image, but instead of using a direct image, you use one that is analogous to it or symbolic of it or for it – as long as it's meaningful to you in that way. So you can use as symbols colour, number, sound and pattern as well as any abstruse intellectual or allegorical constructions you may want to use or test.

Colour A typical example of the use of colour is the Mager disc (invented by the French dowser Henri Mager), and though the idea and his use of it are part of traditional dowsing, I think it's better in this section. Mager originally designed the disc to test the potability of water. Some interpretations of the colours are shown in Fig. 20 – though note that as usual the meanings of specific colours may vary from one dowser to another.

Make a disc yourself from plastic, painted wood, or card-

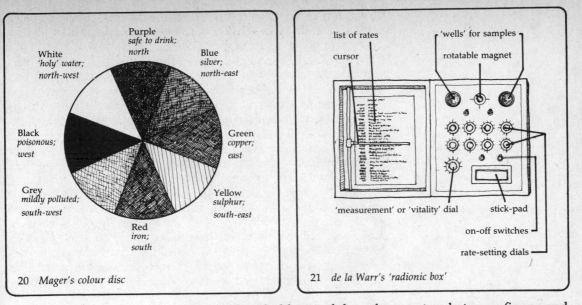

20   *Mager's colour disc*

Purple
*safe to drink;
north*

White
*'holy' water;
north-west*

Blue
*silver;
north-east*

Black
*poisonous;
west*

Green
*copper;
east*

Grey
*mildly polluted;
south-west*

Yellow
*sulphur;
south-east*

Red
*iron;
south*

21   *de la Warr's 'radionic box'*

list of rates

'wells' for samples

cursor

rotatable magnet

'measurement' or 'vitality' dial

stick-pad

on-off switches

rate-setting dials

board. Then hold one of the colour sectors between finger and thumb, and hold a pendulum (in the other hand) over some sample of food, such as a cup of coffee. Note if and how the reaction of the pendulum changes as you turn the disc from sector to sector, using different colours as your symbolic samples. After some practice and comparison, you will be able to use the colours as samples to look for specific qualities of – in this case – foods.

These samples can have other qualitative uses in, for instance, assessment of the activity of specific organs in medical diagnosis, as described in some books on medical dowsing. It's also interesting to compare the meanings of the colours here with the meanings ascribed to them in colour 'theories' such as those of Goethe or Steiner.

Sound   Can be used experimentally, or else specifically, as in fringe medicine. If you just want to experiment, try dowsing anywhere while listening to different kinds of sound through headphones (via a cassette recorder). See if different kinds of sounds and music act as filters for different objects or influences.

The medical uses of sound, and the dowsing tests for it, are very precise and detailed, and I haven't got room to discuss them here. As far as I know they do work, often very effectively. If you want to know more about it, look it up in some of the books on medical dowsing listed in the Appendix.

Number and proportion The best-known use of number and proportion in dowsing is on the early radionic 'Black Boxes' (see Fig. 21). Specific sequences of numbers are set up on the dials of the 'box' as qualitative samples for organs, pathogens and so on, with some organic sample such as a blood-spot being used as a sample of the patient as a whole. The actual dowsing instrument is either a 'stick-pad' on the 'box', or else a pendulum. The pseudo-electronic circuitry of the 'box' doesn't appear to be essential – I know one operator who justs writes down the numbers on a piece of paper – but it does seem to be a help to some operators.

Numbers can also be used as dowsing samples in working on 'fringe' areas such as numerology, gematria, 'sacred geometry', and so on. Again, the numbers can be set up on a modified radionic box, written down on a piece of paper, or just held as an image in the mind.

Pattern Pattern is used as well as number on some of the later radionic 'boxes', notably Tansley's, which is shown in Fig. 22. The concern with pattern seems to be derived from the medical version of the Hindu concepts of 'chakras' and 'energy bodies', which Tansley's box uses in preference to the older semi-physical system. More about this later.

Analogy and allegory You can also use as a sample anything which to you symbolizes what you're looking for, either by association, or by analogy or allegory. It doesn't matter in the slightest what the object *is*, what matters is what it *means* to you at the moment – so a rose can imply Aunt Mabel, a penny could imply water, and a photograph of a deer (a hart) Hertfordshire. It's entirely up to you.

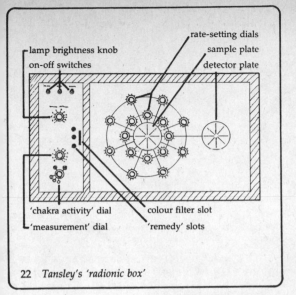

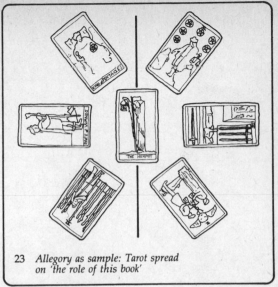

lamp brightness knob

on-off switches

rate-setting dials

sample plate

detector plate

'chakra activity' dial

'measurement' dial

colour filter slot

'remedy' slots

22 Tansley's 'radionic box'

23 Allegory as sample: Tarot spread on 'the role of this book'

It could also be argued that the Tarot, the *I Ching* and other divinatory tools are dowsing techniques using symbolic analogy and allegory as samples for specific states of mind and situation. I have used both the Tarot and the *I Ching* for dowsing purposes before now, and they do work as such.

Mental questions, or the 'Yes'/'No' system

While all the earlier techniques could be used with any instrument, the mental-questions system is effectively for the pendulum only, for only the pendulum has the necessary range of reactions, precision and speed of reply. The idea is that you ask yourself – or the pendulum – a series of questions which can be answered by 'Yes' or 'No', or, as I'll explain later, a number or an indicated direction.

The first thing you have to do is to identify what movement of the pendulum signifies 'Yes' for you, and what 'No'. For some people 'No' is a neutral oscillation, and 'Yes' any gyration; but if you can train it to do so, I think you'll find it more useful if you get the pendulum to gyrate one way for 'Yes', and the other for

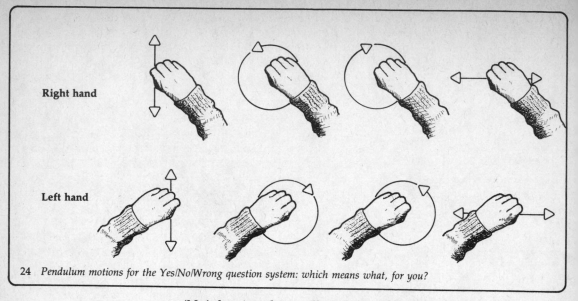

Right hand

Left hand

24   *Pendulum motions for the Yes/No/Wrong question system: which means what, for you?*

'No', leaving the oscillation for 'Neutral'. So try this now:

- Take a pendulum. Set it swinging in neutral, in oscillation.

- Think of a 'positive', think of a 'Yes', and impress the pendulum with your intention that it should gyrate in the direction for 'Yes'. *Don't force it to go in any direction* – let it decide which way *it* wants to gyrate.

- Now do the same for 'negative', 'No'. If they both turn out to be the same direction, try again, with the same or the other hand.

This may take a little practice to sort out, and you may have to 'train' the pendulum to work in this way. Note that for some people these reactions have a nasty habit of changing, so do check them from time to time. For me, 'Yes' is clockwise in the right hand, and 'No' anti-clockwise; they are reversed in the other hand. And since I prefer to leave the neutral strictly as

'Neutral' – 'non-committal', if you like – I've trained my use of the pendulum to add in another reaction, an oscillation at right angles to the neutral. If this comes up when I'm doing some kind of an analysis, it implies that I'm on the wrong track – 'the question asked is such that to answer either Yes or No would be wrong'. There's no word in English that quite covers this, apart from de Bono's invented word 'po'; about the only equivalent I can think of is the Japanese word 'mu'.

With these reactions sorted out for yourself – and I must repeat that they may well be different for you – you can ask the pendulum any question which it can answer within the range of its reactions – and that includes a vast range of possible qualitative, quantitative, positional and directional questions, operating in either normal or non-normal space-time. Note that the way you frame the question will affect the answer – if you ask a woolly question, you'll get a woolly answer. In particular don't make the all-too-easy mistake of asking a double question – 'Is it red or blue?' – to which the answer 'Yes' is meaningless, or a question like 'Is this negative?', to which a 'No' gyration could also mean 'negative', in other words, 'Yes'. But practice at this general method, this 'Yes'/'No' method – it's the most flexible tool you have.

7 Position and direction

These techniques fall into two groups, those which operate within the physical world, and those which operate partly or wholly outside it. It's the first group only which I'll be describing here; the second group, which includes techniques for map dowsing and for operating in time, I've left until Chapter 9, because the checks and controls for the two groups are somewhat different. But more about that later: back to the more 'ordinary' techniques for now.

Position relative to the surface

Traditionally the instrument is assumed to react only when it is directly over the object, the object being directly below the *instrument*, not the operator, when the reaction occurs. With a spring rod the object is supposed to be directly below the tip of the rod; with angle rods, below their crossing point. This is quite adequate for the basic work you've done so far, but it is somewhat imprecise, mainly because of the parallax error caused by the distance between the instrument and the ground. In other words, it isn't easy to see clearly what's happening. For serious work you'll need to be as precise as you can – so instead of the traditional assumption, use your body to mark the object's position.

The body as a marker: *feet*

The first technique here, which you can do with any instrument, is to use the *leading edge of the leading foot* as your marker. As each foot is brought forward as you walk along, its leading edge – or whatever other point you care to use – becomes your marker. With a little practice you should be able to pinpoint an object or the edge of a pipe with this method to around half an inch – that's an accuracy to aim at, anyway. You can expect to be rather

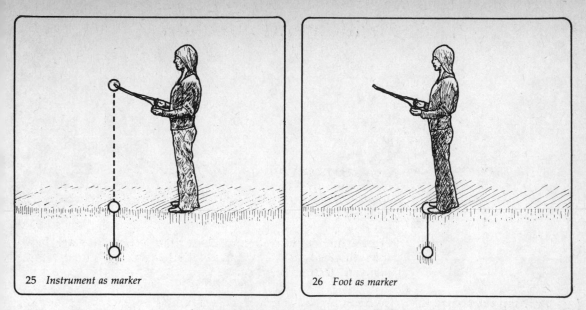

25 *Instrument as marker*

26 *Foot as marker*

less accurate when following the line of a pipe or stream, but if necessary you should be able to mark out the line to within a couple of inches either side of its true line. It isn't as difficult as it sounds: you just need to watch your instrument and your feet with a little care, that's all.

Fingers For more precise work, or for situations where you can't use your feet – as in tracing a leak in a vertical water pipe – use the tips of the fingers of one hand as your marker. You'll have to use a pendulum as your instrument for this, of course. You should be able to get the accuracy down to a quarter of an inch or less with this method, though that will depend on what you want to do. If you need to be still more precise, you can use the tip of some hand-held probe – a pencil or a pin, for instance – as the marker: this is particularly useful in map-dowsing, as I'll explain later.

Hands Another pendulum-only technique: use the flat palm of the free hand as the marker, a marker of an edge rather than a point.

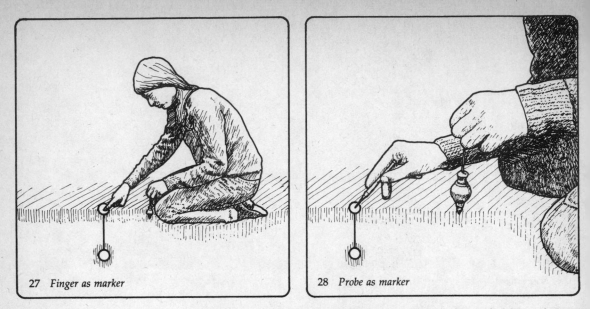

27 *Finger as marker*

28 *Probe as marker*

This isn't used much: its main use is in work on 'fields', particularly in trying to establish their effective size. You could use it to study electrostatic or magnetic fields, but since conventional instruments are more reliable – and safer in this context – there isn't all that much point. But various kinds of 'field' – analogous to electrostatic fields – seem to surround everything animate, and even some things inanimate, such as standing stones. I suppose these could be the so-called 'auras'. From my various experiments I've found the effective edge of one 'field' to extend (in humans, at least) from a few inches to several feet outward, measured from the shoulder, the size varying, apparently, with the person's state of health and other factors. Try it for yourself: bring the palm of your free hand slowly in towards the shoulder of someone you can 'borrow' for a few minutes, or else in towards the trunk of a tree. Note if and when the pendulum reacts, as you keep the idea of the 'field' in mind.

Width of a pipe or stream To find the width of a pipe or stream by a positional method you will need to be as accurate as possible. This precision comes

29 *Hand as marker for human 'field'*

30 *Animate 'field' round a tree and a sapling*

most readily if you watch your instruments carefully. You may have found already that as you approach the line, your angle rods begin to close, or your pendulum slightly changes its axis of swing – as though thinking, considering whether to gyrate – or the tip of your spring rod moves slightly from the horizontal: this is your 'early warning system'. Encourage this slight movement; train the instruments (and yourself) so that there is a short delay period, a warning period, before the instrument reacts sharply and precisely at the point. The reaction-point, marked by your feet or your hands, will be where the rods are *fully* crossed; where the pendulum is gyrating (gyrating smoothly in a circle, not in a series of ellipses); where the rod finally and sharply springs up, or down.

To find that width, you need to mark both sides of the line. Using any instrument, come at the line from one side, and then from the other. Mark the *first* edge of the line from each side; the distance between the two sets of marks should be the width of the pipe or stream. If you find that you've got a negative width

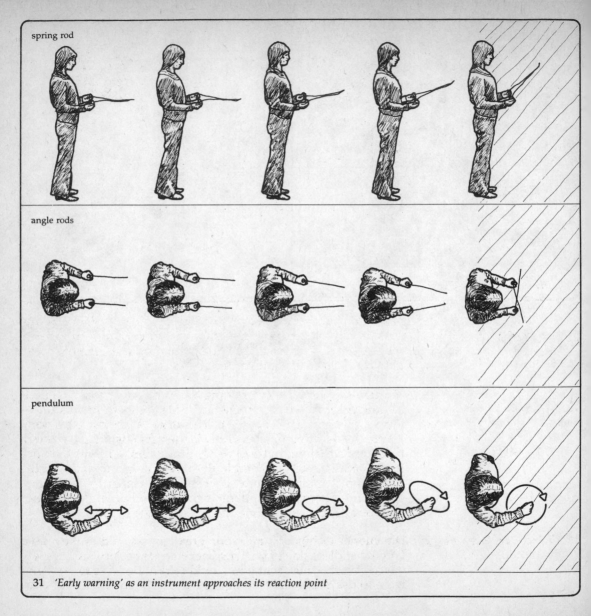

spring rod

angle rods

pendulum

31 *'Early warning' as an instrument approaches its reaction point*

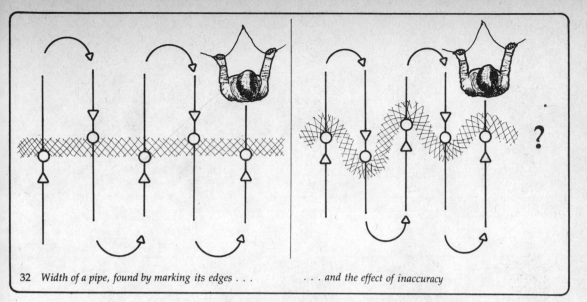

of line, in that the points overlap, you need a little more practice! This problem is more likely to come up when using a spring rod, for reasons I've already explained. But common sense should tell you to cross at right angles to the line.

There's a simpler way of doing this with angle rods or a pendulum. As you come up to the line, note the instrument's warning signals and slow down to a shuffle. As before, the point where the instrument reacts fully is the first edge. Note or mark that edge as before, but *keep going*, don't stop. At some distance further on, the rods will suddenly start to open out again, or the pendulum's motion return to erratic ellipses or to oscillation. The point where this happens is the second edge; the distance between the two should be the width of the pipe.

Direction to an object   Directional techniques are your great time-savers – they save you the endless slog of walking backwards and forwards, slowly quartering the sites, that you would otherwise have to do if you were to use positional techniques alone. The idea is to use your

71

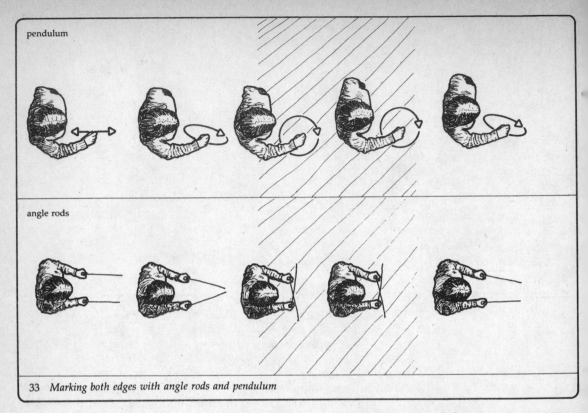

pendulum

angle rods

33   *Marking both edges with angle rods and pendulum*

instruments to point out the direction of the object's position-relative-to-the-surface, and then find that position either by triangulation or by 'tracking'. The choice of technique depends partly on the instrument, and partly on what you want to do.

Triangulation   By using two or more bearings (from two corners of a field, perhaps) given by your instruments, you should be able to pinpoint the position of an object by triangulation. There are two methods you can use for this: the 'turn' and the 'scan'. Since both techniques are done from a standing position, they aren't really suitable for use with angle rods, for you'll probably find

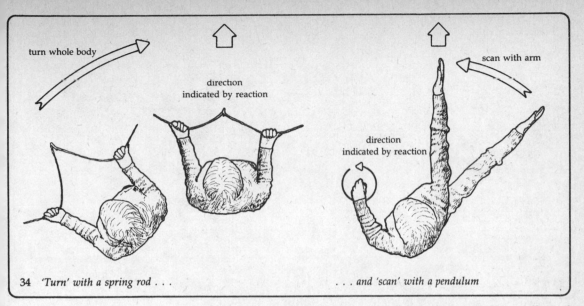

turn whole body

direction
indicated by reaction

scan with arm

direction
indicated by reaction

34 *'Turn' with a spring rod . . .*   *. . . and 'scan' with a pendulum*

that the rods will move clumsily when you're standing still, and will only move smoothly when you are moving too.

Turn   This is the only practical directional technique with a spring rod; you can also use a pendulum. Hold the instrument in the neutral position. Turn round slowly on the spot, keeping in mind that you want the instrument to react when you directly face the position of the object. Keep the idea 'Which way is the object?' in mind. Mark the line indicated. Now repeat as necessary elsewhere on the field; the object's position (relative to the surface, as usual) should be the point where all the lines converge.

Scan   This is a variation of the turn technique, using a pendulum and the free arm or hand. Swing the pendulum in neutral. Proceed as for the turn, but move your free arm rather than your whole body: use your arm to point out a direction, and the pendulum to tell you when it's the right one. Some dowsers prefer to use a hand-held stick, or some other kind of spike or probe, with

35 'Scan' using (a) a finger as pointer, (b) the edge of a hand as pointer, (c) a rod as pointer

which to point out the direction: I don't think it's essential at all, although sometimes it can be helpful, simply by extending the effective length of the line-of-sight marker. Then as before, mark the directions given and construct a triangulation to the object.

Tracking In other words, following the track implied by the directional reactions of the angle rods or pendulum until a positional reaction occurs, indicating the position of the object.

Angle rods As usual, relax for a moment. Bring the rods up to the neutral position. Walk forward, keeping in mind the question 'Which way is the object?' The rods should swing, parallel, to point out a direction. Turn and walk along the line they indicate. Follow any indicated changes in direction; if the rods don't move, keep walking straight ahead. Keep your mind on the job! Don't be surprised if you find you're wandering about a bit, for a 'hunting' or over-correcting tendency isn't unusual, especially in the early stages of practice. But at some point the rods should cross

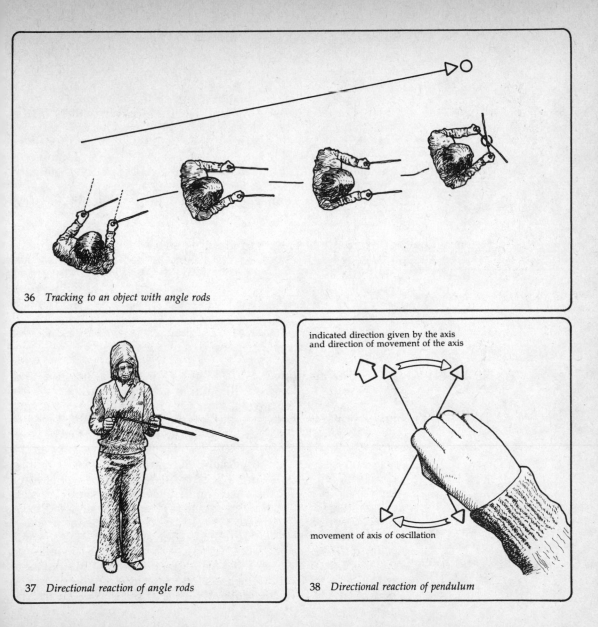

36 *Tracking to an object with angle rods*

37 *Directional reaction of angle rods*

indicated direction given by the axis
and direction of movement of the axis

movement of axis of oscillation

38 *Directional reaction of pendulum*

over sharply, and probably suddenly: that point should be the position of the object.

Pendulum The procedure with a pendulum is the same, using the pendulum's directional and positional reactions this time. The directional reaction here is a change in the axis of oscillation, the direction implied being given by the new axis and by the direction that the axis has moved from its original neutral position (see Fig. 38). Follow the line implied by the axis; follow any changes in direction, as with the rods. At some point the pendulum's movement should change sharply to gyration: as before, that reaction-point should mark the position of the object.

Direction of flow I've found that on crossing a water-flow there is an automatic tendency for the rods or pendulum to point to its *downflow*, especially if the question 'Which way is it flowing?' is kept in mind. For anything other than water – current 'flow' in power cables, for instance – that question does seem to be essential, though it doesn't seem to be so for water itself. Having found the direction of flow, you can then trace the course of the stream, or whatever, by using a tracking technique.

Tracking a course Use either instrument and follow the indicated direction and any changes in direction. Keep in mind a question like 'Which way does this thing flow?'; in the case of a flow, you can follow the course *upstream* instead by keeping in mind 'Which way is the *reverse* flow?' You can track the line or course of any linear object in this way. Note that you will almost certainly appear to 'hunt' or overcorrect, especially on a line that is more than a couple of feet wide, so don't be surprised if what is supposed to be a linear pipe, for instance, appears to follow a wildly zigzag course (see Fig. 39). Watch your instrument carefully, and with practice you should be able to track the *edge* of some linear object to within a couple of inches. But do beware of expectations and of jumping to conclusions: beware of thinking 'Ah! That looks like the line down there!' It may be the right line, or it may be a wrong one; it may just be 'noise'. So watch what you're doing, both mentally and physically. Keep your mind on your instru-

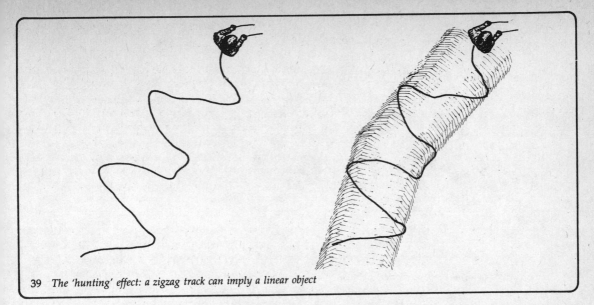

39 *The 'hunting' effect: a zigzag track can imply a linear object*

ment, on the ground at your feet, and on the problem at hand: don't go mentally sailing off twenty feet away, or you'll end up – literally – going round in circles.

Which brings me to another point: if you're tracking a stream – as opposed to a pipe – don't be surprised if from time to time you *do* find yourself going round in tight circles. Streams will form these 'knots' for some unclear reason, and catches like these are part of the subtleties of tracking. As usual, the effects and meanings of these subtleties vary according to what you're tracking and what instrument you're using.

Some notes on tracking: *pendulum* Suppose, to take the example of a stream, you're tracking it with a pendulum and you find it turns sharp left – and keeps turning, till you find yourself going round and round on the spot. What do you do now? First of all: *stop*. Now start the pendulum again, and ask it – and yourself – 'Which way does the stream go now?' Don't be surprised if the pendulum gives you more than one direction, changing its axis of swing from one line to another.

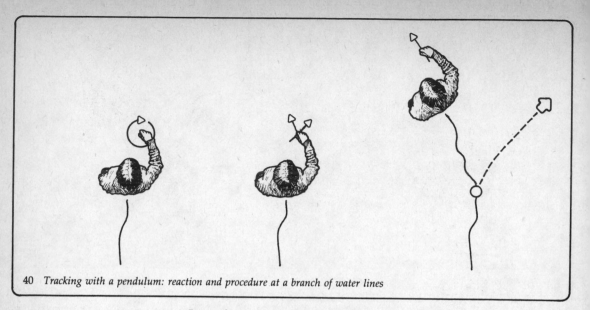

40 *Tracking with a pendulum: reaction and procedure at a branch of water lines*

Just choose one direction, note for future reference that the stream branched at that point, and carry on tracking the branch you've chosen (see Fig. 40). These 'knots' of water lines do some other strange things, as Guy Underwood found out – but more about that later.

Back to tracking with a pendulum. You're going along as before, and suddenly the pendulum starts gyrating. Assuming that you're keeping your mind on the job, and so haven't 'found' something that you were casually thinking about, it should mean either that the stream has branched again (in which case handle that as in the last paragraph) or else that another stream, or something similar, crosses the line of the stream at that point but at a different depth. And so on: you have to use your ingenuity and your intuition to work out what is going on.

Angle rods   Angle rods have an advantage over a pendulum in tracking, in that they can tell what is actually happening at a branch-point. If

78

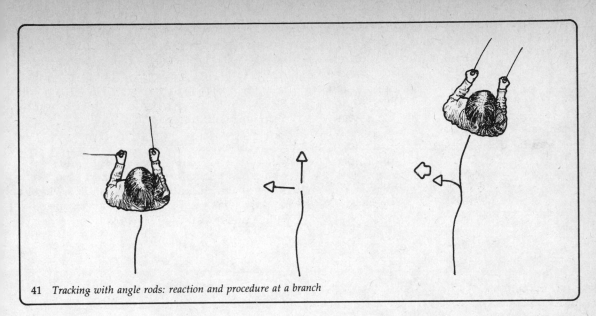

41 *Tracking with angle rods: reaction and procedure at a branch*

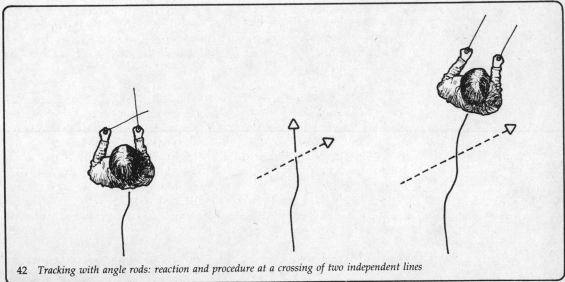

42 *Tracking with angle rods: reaction and procedure at a crossing of two independent lines*

the left-hand rod turns off to the left while the other continues straight ahead, the stream has a left-hand branch; if the right-hand rod crosses the left-hand one, which itself remains pointing straight ahead, there is another stream or pipe flowing from right to left at a different level; and vice versa, of course (see Figs. 41 and 42). At least, that's what I've trained my rods to do – see what you can get yours to do for you.

Mental questions again   As in the qualitative techniques, you can also 'ask' the pendulum positional and directional questions: 'Is it this field?', 'Is it north of here?', 'Which way is it from here?', and so on. The same rules apply as before, in that a woolly question will get a woolly answer; in particular, avoid double-questions and double-negatives. Plan your questions carefully!

8 Quantities

Once again the techniques vary according to what you're trying to do and what instrument you're using. There are two groups of techniques: those which can give quantitative answers directly, and those which have to give those answers indirectly or by analogy. I'll deal with the former group first.

Instrument-indicated reactions
The sharpness and apparent strength of the instrument's reaction are your first indicators of size, but in practice these can only be used as a very rough guide. Due to a whole range of factors, even an experienced dowser's sensitivity may vary a great deal from second to second, let alone over a period of hours or days, so it just isn't safe to rely on the strength of the reaction alone – and since they are personal, the terms 'weak reaction' and 'strong reaction' will probably be meaningless to anyone else. But by using some kind of system which can measure the apparent strength of the reaction, you can use its variations precisely and meaningfully – and you should find that your sensitivity will adapt automatically to the system's needs. Three examples of this are the use of graduated angle rods, the use of a separation-type rod, and the method of counting the number of gyrations made by a pendulum.

Graduated angle rods
These are ordinary angle rods, but with one or both rods marked at regular intervals along the long arm. You can use some other scale – trigonometrical, logarithmic – if need be. The rods are used in the usual way – though you'll need to watch that your hands don't wander apart and change the effective scale – the only difference being that you do not want them to close *completely* on crossing a pipe or stream. Instead, keep in

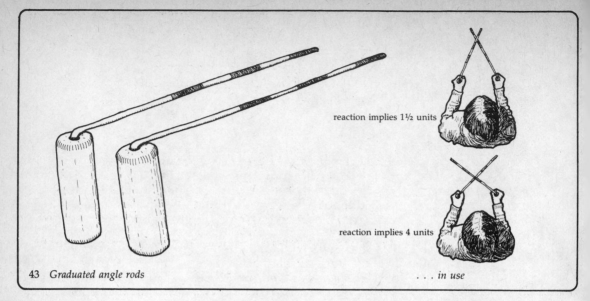

reaction implies 1½ units

reaction implies 4 units

43　*Graduated angle rods* .... *in use*

mind that you want them to close so that the degree of closure, and thus the point marked on the scale, implies the size (or rate of flow or whatever else you're after) of the pipe or stream. Note that the marks of the scale on the rods are meaningless in themselves: you have to assign meaning, some kind of scale, to the marks before you can use them meaningfully for any purpose. So before you start, assign units to the marks – feet, inches, cubic feet per second – and a scale or order – one mark for one foot, five feet, a hundred feet. More about this shortly.

Separation-type rod I've only mentioned the separation rod before in passing rather than in detail. It works by measuring the varying separation of the hands, a simple system of levers acting as an amplifier to put the movement onto a dial. It is used in the same way as the graduated angle rods. And as with the rods, remember to assign a scale of units – and thus a meaning – to the figures on the scale, according to what you're testing for.

Pendulum gyrations Use the pendulum in the usual way, but state in your mind that

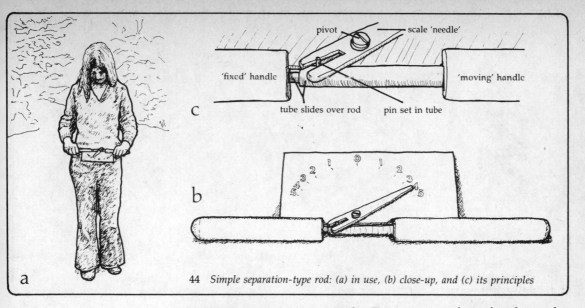

44 *Simple separation-type rod: (a) in use, (b) close-up, and (c) its principles*

you're using it quantitatively. For your numbers for the scale, use the number of gyrations of the pendulum, assigning a unit and order of units to each gyration. I've found that it doesn't matter at what point I start counting – I can start counting after the bob has gone round two or three times, and still end up with the same result – but I think it's easiest to count the number of full gyrations from the point where and when the bob first moves *in a circle* to when it drops back to steep ellipses or to oscillation.

Unlike the other two instruments, you have a choice of the type of scale. You can either take a fixed number of gyrations – say, ten – as your equivalent of the rods' 'full-scale deflection', and choose a suitable scale of units to match; or else you can use an open-ended scale, and just keep counting until the pendulum decides to stop. Choose your order of units for the open scale carefully though, or you may find yourself trying to count hundreds or thousands of gyrations! The closed scale is useful for when you want to get a rough idea of size, and for finding

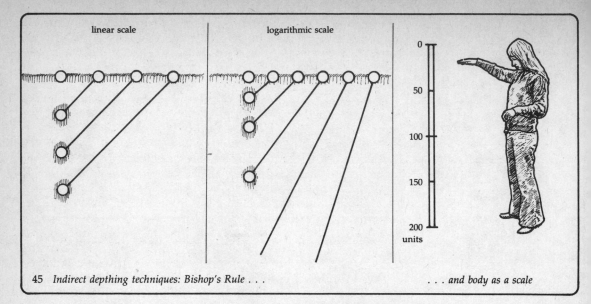

logarithmic scale

0

50

100

150

200
units

45 *Indirect depthing techniques: Bishop's Rule . . .*   *. . . and body as a scale*

percentages and such like; but the open scale is more adaptable and flexible, and usually more precise.

Indirect techniques   A number of quantitative techniques use an external scale, and thus work indirectly rather than directly. One example of this is the Bishop's Rule for depthing, which I described earlier, in which the distance *out* from the original reaction point is assumed to be equivalent to the distance *down* – a horizontal scale is substituted for a vertical one. But there are other versions of the Rule that you can use: for instance, instead of using a linear scale you could use a logarithmic one, so that one foot out equals one foot down, two feet out equals ten feet down, three feet out a hundred, four a thousand, and so on.

Another way is to use your height as an analogue of the depth – the level of the top of your head being equivalent to ground level, and the level of your feet being equivalent to, say, two hundred feet down. Hold a spring rod at the level of the top of your head; alternatively, use the hand-and-pendulum technique and use your palm to mark the level. Slowly bring the instrument or marker down and note the level at which the instrument reacts – in this example, the neck 'is' thirty feet down, the waist a hundred feet, and so on in proportion.

Another method uses a pendulum and a ruler. Run a finger of the free hand along the ruler until the pendulum reacts: the point on the ruler, combined with the scale of units you've assigned to it, should give you the quantitative information you need. But remember that in all these techniques the critical thing is the scale of units that you use. So before I go any further, I'd better talk about scales.

Scales There are three factors in a scale: the units, the order of units, and the type of scale. Firstly, *units*. The units you use arise out of the obvious question of 'What are you looking for?' Distance: feet, inches, yards, miles; centimetres, metres, kilometres. Areas, volumes in imperial or metric units. Weight: grammes or drams; ounces, pounds or kilogrammes; tons or tonnes. Rates of flow: cubic centimetres per second, cubic feet per minute, gallons per day. Time: seconds, minutes, hours, days, weeks, months, years. Temperature, voltage; radiation levels, perhaps; or any other unit you care to think of. So select your units according to what you're doing and what you need.

Once you have the unit, what *order* of units are you using? Is one division on your instrument's scale equivalent to one foot, five feet, ten feet, a hundred feet? Ten gallons per day, a million gallons per day, or only a millilitre a day? One day, a thousand days, a thousand years?

And what *type* of scale are you using? Within either an open or a closed scale a linear type is generally the most useful – the main use of the logarithmic type is in establishing the most suitable order of units to use on a linear scale. There are other types of scale you could use – trigonometrical, algebraic, reciprocal among others – but you'd probably be better off using a set of mathematical tables rather than dowsing.

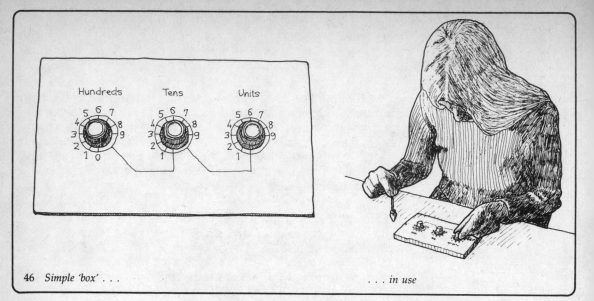

46 *Simple 'box'* . . .   . . . *in use*

So the basic principle of all the quantitative techniques is to preselect the units, order of units and type of scale, and then to use some instrument – either directly or indirectly – to generate a number or a proportion. In any quantitative work assemble the scale according to what you need, and keep it in your mind, rest your mind on it, while you're working.

Quantitative mental questions

All of the above techniques are simple forms of mental questions, since in using them you 'ask for' a quantitative reaction on the instrument. As usual, the best instrument for more complex mental-questions work is the pendulum, used either on its own as described above, or else indirectly, using something else, such as an electronic calculator or a radionic-type 'box', to display numbers for the pendulum to test.

It's easy to build a crude 'box' for this purpose: three old radio knobs (marked 0–9) mounted on a simple wooden frame will be quite adequate. Despite what some writers say, it isn't necessary to include any wires or magnets or other complications (they

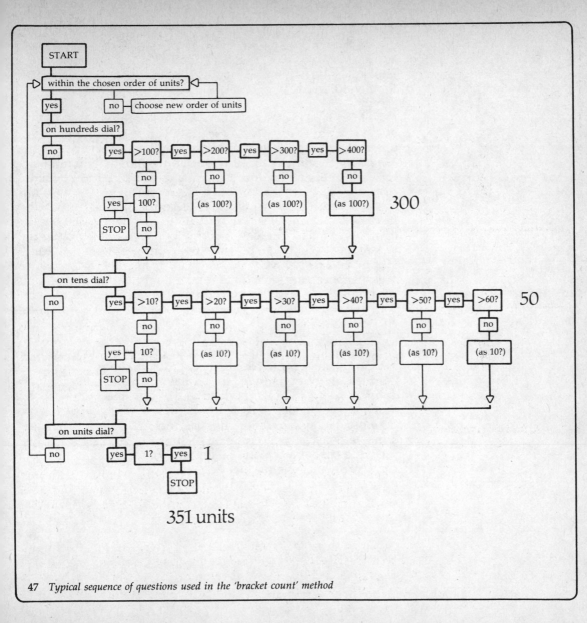

47 *Typical sequence of questions used in the 'bracket count' method*

may help, but that's almost beside the point); but it is useful, as on the 'box' in Fig. 46, to label the dials as for hundreds, tens and units. To use it, hold a pendulum in one hand, turn the knobs with the other, and note at what number on each knob the pendulum reacts.

To take depthing as an example, first ask the pendulum if the depth is within the scale on the units you're using. If not, use a different unit until it is within the scale; if and when it is, you can either turn the dials individually until the pendulum reacts for each one, or else you can use a 'bracket count' method, a stream of 'Is it more than . . . ?'/'Is it less than . . . ?' questions, as shown in Fig. 47. In either case you should end up with a three-figure number – 351, in this case – which implies the depth of the object in feet or decimetres or whatever other unit you're using. So the depth in those units would be 351 feet or 35·1 metres respectively. If you want to use the technique for other applications, just modify the units and order of units accordingly. And you can use this technique in much the same way with other number-generating tools, such as a pocket calculator.

You can also use the 'bracket count' method along with, or instead of, the simple count of gyrations if you're going to use the pendulum on its own. Incidentally, if you watch the pendulum closely in bracket count work, you may find it has a number of subtleties to its reactions. It will rarely move sharply from oscillation to gyration and back again; instead, it will tend to move pensively, carefully, as though saying 'not quite there yet' or 'overshot a bit' and so on. So watch that, for it's useful and worth encouraging. See what you can do.

9 Map and time dowsing
and other techniques in non-normal space-time

These techniques, which operate partly or wholly outside of a physical sense of space and time, are simply logical extensions of the techniques already described. If 'Man is the measure of all things', as the old saying goes, then the body and its senses can be said to define the physical world as we know it. But you have a mind as well as a body, a mind which, by its definition, can operate on but is not strictly part of that physical world.

The limits of the mental world are factors such as paradox and reason, intuition, contemplation, imagination; the physical dimensions of length, breadth, depth and time are included in that mental world – but they are merely part of it, not the whole of it. And since the kind of dowsing I've been describing so far is essentially mental rather than physical – a controlled subjectivity rather than a physical 'objectivity' – there is no reason why in using it you *must* operate solely within the confines of the physical definition of the world. It may be *simpler* or *easier* to operate physically, as indeed it usually is; but that doesn't mean that it's the *only* way you can operate, does it?

But when working in these areas be careful not to carry over the assumptions you use automatically in working physically, for here you are dealing with a different world governed by different rules. It is essential to realize that you aren't dealing with 'real', tangible objects at all, but only with a shadowy assortment of information sources, and all of them of dubious reliability at that. The idea is to somehow extract meaning and usefulness from that information. And since operation in these areas is by definition subjective, *the reliability of any operation is*

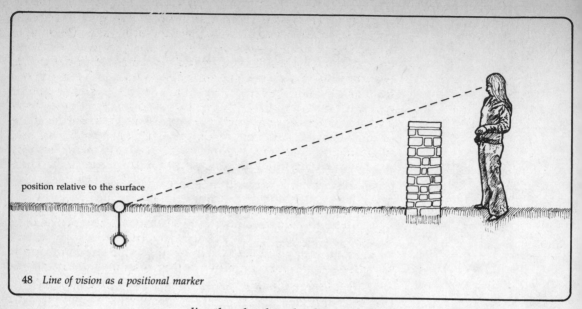

position relative to the surface

48 *Line of vision as a positional marker*

directly related to the degree of psychological control (see Chapter 4 again). So beware – it's all too easy to fool yourself!

And with that warning, on to the techniques themselves.

Vision as a marker In all the techniques described in Chapter 7 you can substitute either 'the point you are looking at' or 'the direction in which you are looking' for the physical markers and pointers described there. You'll find it easier to do this if you imagine yourself walking over the area, imagine yourself holding a marker at the point you're looking at. This 'vision as a marker' technique is particularly useful if some obstruction (such as a fence or a wall) prevents you from using the earlier techniques. Simple marking of distance or position is, with some practice, quite easy; but note that any complex tracking will make hefty demands on your mental agility and control, and will be anything but easy.

Positional samples As opposed to the qualitative use of 'samples' described in

Chapter 6. These can be anything which can give or imply a position, a place, a situation in space and/or in time. The sample is used simply and solely as a source of spatial or temporal information – it doesn't matter what the sample *is*, but what it is used to *mean*. So almost anything that comes to hand will do: from an Ordnance Survey map to a scribbled sketch; a photograph old or new; a set of engravings or drawings; some object such as an arrowhead which can be traced to a particular place or time, or both; anything, or almost anything. You can see that many of the qualitative samples discussed earlier can also be used as positional ones. In this sort of work the most commonly used sample is a map, and so I'll start with map dowsing.

Map dowsing   Always remind yourself that you're using the map as *referential information*, as an aid to finding a particular place, rather than using it as an object in its own right. In other words, you aren't so much dowsing the map itself as dowsing the information it supplies and implies. So don't bother orienting the map precisely north-south, or whatever – mixing semi-physical methods with non-physical ones will only add unnecessary confusion.

When working on the map visualize yourself, if you can, walking around in the area it describes. See if you can find the overall 'feel' of the area; build up the intuitive side of the operation so as to build up the sense of meaning and purpose. The positional techniques used on the map are much the same as those for on-site work: the area or grid method, the co-ordinate or triangulation method, and the tracking method.

Area method   The area method is the equivalent of quartering a site in on-site work. For this you need to have some kind of grid on the map: Ordnance Survey maps already have them, but on other maps mark one in lightly in pencil. Starting with large grid squares – say the ten-kilometre squares on a 1" OS map – run through them in sequence, asking 'Is the object in this square?' for each square in turn. Assuming that the pendulum does react for one square, break that square down into smaller squares – the one-kilometre squares on the OS map – and repeat. And repeat as is necessary and practical with progressively smaller and smaller

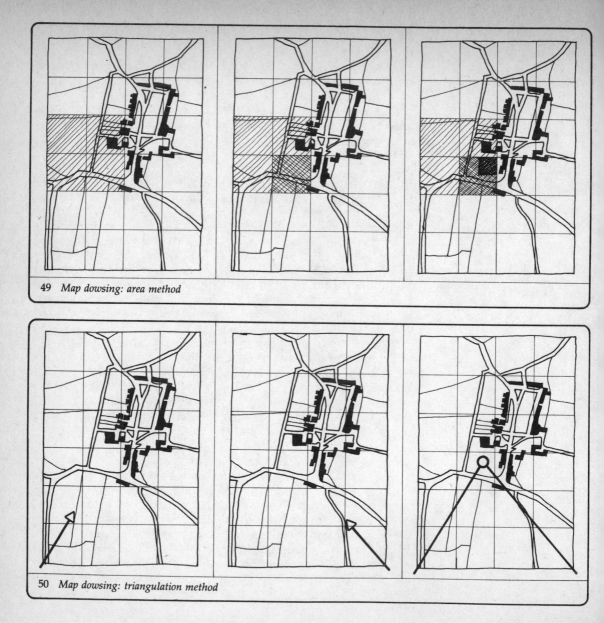

49   *Map dowsing: area method*

50   *Map dowsing: triangulation method*

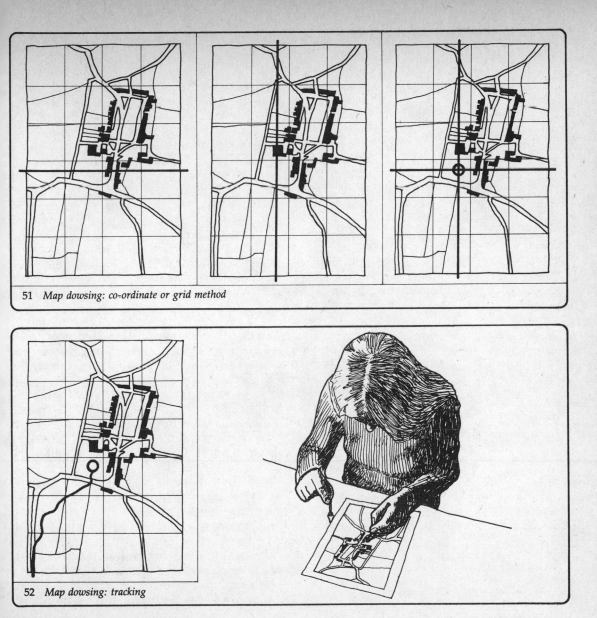

51 *Map dowsing: co-ordinate or grid method*

52 *Map dowsing: tracking*

squares, until you can find the position of the object as precisely as possible.

Co-ordinate method There are two ways of doing this. One is to choose two or more arbitrary points and proceed as for on-site triangulation, asking 'In which direction is the object?' from each of those points. The directional reactions – of a pendulum only, in this case, since other instruments are impractical for map dowsing – will give a set of bearings which should converge on the position of the object as implied by the map.

Another method is to use the co-ordinate structure of the map itself – the grid. Run one hand down a north-south side of the map with a pendulum in the other hand, and with the question 'Where (on the grid) is the object?' in mind. Note if and where the pendulum reacts – that's your 'northing'. Now do the same on an east-west edge so as to find the 'easting'. The point on the map given by these two co-ordinates, the map reference, should be the implied position of the object.

Tracking Tracking on a map can only be done with a pendulum, with all that instrument's attendant advantages and disadvantages. The technique is the same as with on-site tracking, but of course you will be working on a much reduced scale here, and will thus have to be that much more accurate and precise. Note that to get that precision you will need to watch your pendulum's movements very carefully. You can use a finger as your marker in all these techniques, but since on a 1" OS map that's going to cover the equivalent of about a hundred acres, you'll be better off using a pencil or a pin.

Sense and nonsense You can work on any other suitable object or image in the same way as in map dowsing, or else use it in conjunction with a map. But remember that the limit of this kind of work is whether the information derived from the object, the image, the information-source, is meaningful – whether it makes sense – to you, if not necessarily to anyone else. I've found that I can still get 'results' off a sketch-map of a completely imaginary place, which is obviously nonsense (or non-sense) – though Henry de

France, in his *Elements of Dowsing*, describes how he drew a map of what he thought was an imaginary place during a demonstration of the principles of map-dowsing, only to find that in fact he'd described precisely the site of a new well at his visitor's farm. . . . But, equally, beware of the more arrogant and dogmatic kind of sceptic who will 'prove' to himself that dowsing is 'nonsense' by the childish but ever-popular game of sending you a fake map. Few things could be more calculated to destroy a beginner's self-confidence!

Dowsing in time

If you can work outside the physical definition of space, then you can also work outside of and through the physical definition of time – the theory's as simple as that. And, pleasantly, so is the practice. There are two main ways of working, used for different purposes: working *to* a point in time, as in determining the age of an archaeological object; and working *from* a point in time, as in finding the variation over the seasons of the rate of flow of a stream. But before I describe the respective techniques, I'd better deal with a problem that always arises from them: the inherent paradoxes in and unreliability of prediction.

The paradoxes of prediction

Every system of prediction – be it dowsing, astrology, divination, the Tarot or whatever – is trapped in an irresolvable web of paradoxes. In operating to or from a different point in time, the effective place of operation within time is shifted from 'real-time' (clock or physical time), through a state of timelessness, and back into physical time again – or, rather, what *appears* to be physical time. The path from 'real-time' to that apparent point could be called a 'line of time', or a time-line: and there are an infinite number of time-lines possible, since they are all imaginary (though useful, of course). The problem is to find which line is the 'true' one. Now, as a friend put it, 'working backward is fairly straightforward': the time-line to any point in the *historical* past is defined by our sense of history. In effect, our sense of history controls that shift through timelessness, fixing the time-line of the apparent past. Thus any operator with a certain degree of skill and practice should, when working backward in time, end up with roughly the same results as everyone else: and this is in fact what happens.

But the same cannot be said of prediction or, to some extent, of working with the pre-historic past. Unlike working backward in historical time, there is no history of the future: there is nothing to define the 'true' time-line. The result is that every operator comes up with a different concept of the future, and all and none of them are 'true'. There will be some agreement at any given time, but the best that can be achieved is an image of the most *probable* future, the most probable according to the information available at that given point in real-time – and even then the act of observing the future changes the probabilities of different time-lines, too, by another related set of paradoxes. And since all that information has also to be filtered through the operator's conscious and unconscious assumptions and expectations, you can see that the 'most probable future' will be constantly changing.

Thus in working with time remember that you're dealing solely with infinite sets of information, and that that information is subject to an infinite number of possible interpretations. It's all too easy to see what you want or expect to see: so beware – while it's interesting to look into what seems to be the future, *never assume that what you see is 'the truth'*.

Dowsing to a time
To determine the age of an object or the date or time of its manufacture, use or operation, frame the respective problem ('age', 'date' or whatever) in your mind and proceed by using any quantitative technique you care to use. The pendulum-gyrations and pendulum-and-box methods are probably the most useful here, though no doubt you could devise some modification of the Bishop's Rule that would equate distance with displacement in time.

Dowsing from a time
For most dowsing purposes you don't need to consider your effective operating position in time, as your body and its senses will determine that position automatically according to the rules of real-time. But for some kinds of work it's useful to override that automatic process and to operate from an apparently different position in time. Two examples of this are in establishing the probable variation of flow of a stream over a period of time, and

in archaeological survey work. In both cases the required operating date or position in time must be framed and held in the mind with a high degree of care, for there seems (not all that surprisingly) to be an automatic tendency to return to operating in real-time – and that really does make a mess of the results!

In the case of the stream, it's best to frame and operate from a sequence of different positions in time, both backward and forward. The probability of accurate prediction is higher than usual here, because many of the factors affecting the flow of the stream are cyclical or seasonal; in fact the real problems in prediction are the 'random' and multiple-variable factors, because they're impossible to allow for in detail.

In archaeological work you can either frame the date you want in your mind, or use some suitable object (such as a piece of contemporary pottery, or an old photograph or drawing) as a temporal sample, as referential information for the date. Select a date or sequence of dates to operate from in this way, and then proceed, using the usual positional, directional, qualitative and quantitative techniques as you need. More about this in Chapter 13.

Psychometry Psychometry is effectively an extreme form of dowsing from a time. Holding an old object, photograph or drawing, the idea is to try to get an overall 'feel' of the time and situation the sample represents, as though images, sights, sounds, smells, emotions and so on are stored 'inside' it. You don't need an instrument for this – the instrument you use is yourself. Just handle the object; feel its shape, its surface; listen to it, to the 'sounds that are no sounds' surrounding it; close your eyes and mentally go inside it. Forget about what the object *is*, concern yourself with what it *means*, or appears to mean; and don't try too hard, just allow any impressions to arise 'of their own accord'. As a beginner you'll probably sense nothing that seems out of the ordinary and will possibly think the whole thing is rather pointless anyway, but keep at it. It doesn't take long to learn to recognize the clear impressions that do arise – if you let them. Remember, though, that the information arising out of this is subjective, not objective – don't fall into the trap of thinking that it's 'the truth'. In experimental work psychometry can be a surprisingly valuable information source once you get the knack of handling it, and it's great fun, too. It's worth a try, if nothing else.

Problems and controls   The main problem with all non-physical work is that since it's essentially mental, it's wide open to all the conscious and unconscious intrusions described in Chapter 4. So I must re-emphasize that *if you are unable to keep those intrusions under some semblance of control, your results are going to be useless, or worse.*

So it's safest to practice first on things you can check by other means, and on which it doesn't matter if you make a mistake. In the beginning, at least check your map and time dowsing results by fieldwork, spadework, bookwork, or a combination of the three. And remember that it's *practice* that is the most important part of all in this game!

PART THREE

Applications

10 Introduction to applications

Right, you've ploughed through all those techniques – now what do you *do* with them? The first answer is to practise: until you have some idea of what dowsing *feels* like in practice, you shouldn't rush off and attempt to do anything complicated. Start on something simple first. And the simplest things to start on are what might be called parlour tricks.

Parlour tricks For your next trick you will require the assistance of a member of the audience. . . . Well, don't make it as pompous as that, but you will need to borrow someone – husband, wife, brother, sister or assorted friend – to set up the test part of the 'trick'. The idea is for them to do something which you then have to find out using your various dowsing techniques – a guessing game, in fact.

Start off with a simple positional one, in which the assistant hides something like a coin, which you have to find using positional and directional techniques and with another coin as a sample. Then try a form of 'hide-and-seek', looking for your assistant in a wood or a park.

Use quantitative techniques to find the number of pins or peas under a cup; then try to find the number that someone has written on a piece of paper. Try single-figure numbers first, then move on to multiple-figure numbers.

For a qualitative test, hide three objects (a button, a coin and a cotton reel) under three cups, and try to find which object is under which cup. A simpler qualitative test (one which deals

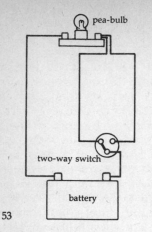

pea-bulb

two-way switch

battery

53

with fields rather than with objects) is the one using the circuit in Fig. 53: four lengths of wire, a two-way switch, a pea-bulb and a battery are all that is needed. The idea is to find which of the two positive wires is carrying the current. If the battery is connected, the bulb will always be lit (assuming that the switch doesn't jam in the middle, of course); the return wire will always be carrying a current, and can thus be used as a reference point. But by twiddling the switch, preferably under cover, your assistant can select which of the positive wires carries the current. You have to decide which one it is.

If you're feeling confident enough to tackle more complex tricks, here are a few suggestions. First, get your assistant to write down the name of some object in the room, and then try to identify it. I usually keep my mind on 'what has been written down' for this, on the *idea* of the words (even though I don't know what the words themselves are) – or, to put it another way, I use the idea of the written words as an abstract or non-physical sample. Try this first with your assistant also keeping his or her mind on what they have written; and then try again – with a different object, of course! – with your assistant deliberately thinking of something else, to 'throw you off the scent' as it were, and see if there is any difference.

Get your assistant to handle one of the objects in the room for a couple of minutes and then put it back exactly in its original position: you then have to find which object was handled. Finally, try and find the object which your assistant is only *thinking* about.

Remember that the idea of all these 'parlour tricks' is to give you, and your assistant if you work in turn, the practical 'feel' of the various techniques. They aren't intended to show everyone how marvellous you are; the idea is to build up your confidence, not your self-importance. If *that's* all you're in this game for, you'll soon find that dowsing has a few traps for the foolish, as I'll explain shortly.

Two-level work In other words, map dowsing followed by ordinary positional work; off-site work followed by on-site work, followed by physical checks to check the results of both the off- and on-site work.

Start with map dowsing. Buy or otherwise acquire the largest scale Ordnance Survey map that you can find of your immediate area – the 1 : 1250 or 1 : 2500 series are best. Most large towns have an OS stockist who should have the sheets for your area, but if you can't get a map that way, chat up a friendly architect or the local Planning Department. Having got the map, use tracking techniques on it to locate the positions and courses of *all* the services – gas, electricity, telephone, mains water, drainage and sewerage – for a number of houses. Note that in some areas the telephone and electricity supply cables come in *above* ground, so you may find it difficult to get any results for these unless you state that you *are* looking for them above ground. There isn't much point in doing all this for just one house, so if your house is miles away from any others, use the map of part of the nearest village, or somewhere else that you know. Go through each service separately, preferably marking them on separate overlays – use tracing or 'layout' paper, or ordinary kitchen greaseproof paper. See what other information you can find on these services – sizes, depths, junctions, taps and so on – and mark it all down. While you're at it, see if you can find any underground streams or the like. In all, it's quite a long job, but it's typical of serious work.

Now repeat as much of this as you can on-site, looking for the individual services and the streams again. After clambering over a few hedges and fences, you'll understand why dowsers use map dowsing such a lot! Mark your results on a new set of overlay sheets – don't compare the two sets of results until you've finished.

Check the results where you can by probing and digging around. Dig with a spade where necessary, but I think you'll find it more fruitful to 'dig' at the various service authorities' offices, nosing through their records (but beware, for their older records are often surprisingly inaccurate and incomplete). The authorities are usually friendly and helpful if you explain what you're trying to do; and since many of them do use amateur dowsers from time to time, you may well be able to help them in return.

If your results do turn out to be all haywire, don't be despondent, because the whole point of this kind of practice is to help you learn from your inevitable mistakes. Mistakes now don't matter, you can happily afford to make them as long as you learn from them; but mistakes later, on a serious job, can be mighty expensive.

And more practice! The suggestions I've given above are only suggestions, no more than that; you don't have to follow them rigidly, in fact it's better if you invent others more or less in line with your own interests. Begin to use dowsing techniques, in their various combinations, to tackle some of the mundane problems that always arise, such as when you've lost your keys; when you have to get in touch with someone and you don't know where they are; when you don't know whether a wire you want to work on is 'live' or not; when you've got to find the break in an underground drain pipe; and so on. Again, it shouldn't matter if your results are wrong, for you can use more conventional tests to check as well; but if they are right, they will have saved you some time and effort. It's best to sort out a sequence of operation before you start, to structure the operation according to the problem's needs.

Structuring an operation Are you looking for something, or have you found something? That's the first point that determines the structure. If it's the former, before you start to look for that 'something', decide and state in your mind *precisely* what it is that you're looking for. Then work out a sequence of operation, breaking down the sequence analytically into the classes of techniques – qualitative, quantitative, positional and directional. Break the operation down into something like the flow-chart described on page 88 and Fig. 47 for using a simple quantitative 'box'. Note that you can use a mixture of techniques simultaneously, especially if you're using the mental-questions system – 'I'm looking for water of drinkable quality at no more than 100 feet down and not less than 1000 gallons available per day.' Split the sequence into off-site and on-site sections; remember that while off-site techniques such as map and time dowsing can save a lot of time and effort later on-site, they aren't as reliable as the on-site techniques themselves. So unless it can't be avoided, *never rely on off-site work alone*.

If you've found something and you don't know what it is – this often happens in research – you have to turn the whole analytic structure upside-down. It's a case of 'I've got an answer – now what on earth was the question?', so you have to try this 'answer', this something, against a series of questions to see which (if any) of them fit. And this is where the 'Yes'/'No'/'Wrong question' system with the pendulum really comes into its own. Starting with questions covering wide generalities, the pendulum should give a string of 'No' or 'Wrong question' answers until you find a question wide enough to include and enclose the original 'something'. Don't force the pace, just let the ideas and images and questions form in your mind of their own accord. This kind of work – 'premise-generation' rather than analytic 'premise-testing', in the terms of conventional logic – is essentially intuitive: the mind must be wide open, with the pendulum simply acting as an indicator, a meter of the state of your mind.

Once you've found a suitable general label, you can then conceptually wobble to and fro from that point, finding more and more specific labels – labels of *classes* of objects – so as to end up with a description of the 'something'. It's rather like the area method of map dowsing, the 'map' in this case being a network of concepts and labels rather than a description of some tangible place. I hope that's clear enough! But like many things in dowsing it may sound complicated when it's described, but it turns out to be simple enough when you actually get down to *doing* it.

Beyond these general descriptions the particular sequence depends on what you want to do, of course. So in the next three chapters I'll be describing briefly a range of common applications for dowsing under the headings of general prospection and analysis, agriculture and medicine, and dowsing and archaeology. These aren't by any means the only applications of dowsing, though, and I've no doubt that in time you'll find plenty more. But before I go on to describe the basics of those applications, there is one topic that *must* be dealt with first: the ethics and limitations of dowsing practice.

Ethics and limitations

As with any practical skill there are a number of points that need to be borne constantly in mind, and which between them form the equivalent of a set of workshop safety regulations and a code of professional practice. Most of these points should be obvious, but just in case they *aren't* obvious, I ought to state them here, because I don't want to be responsible for misguiding you into the one or two traps that do exist in dowsing. This 'code of safe practice' can be reduced to four key points: a matter of *level*, a matter of *responsibility*, a matter of *profit* and a matter of *necessity*.

A matter of level

Or, to be more precise, a matter of level of complexity. It's usually best in any situation to aim for the simplest way of handling that situation (though the simplest way may well not be *apparently* the easiest way), and the same is true of dowsing. The simplest way of doing things in the physical world is to use physical methods – after all, your body is a physical structure that's built to work in that world. So in most situations straight physical working is the lowest level of complexity, lower in level than the 'physical' methods of dowsing, which are themselves lower in level than the 'mental' methods, and so on. In the same way, it's simpler to use an instrument than to dowse without one or to 'use' the instrument without touching it – in other words operating it psychokinetically. All these are *possible*, but the higher the level of complexity, the higher the degree of subjective control required to produce reliable results.

So while it's possible to use dowsing for any problem, with many of them there's simply no point in doing so. Use the lowest practical level in anything other than experimental work: if physical methods and tools – metal detectors, for instance – are available and can do the job reliably, use them. Be realistic!

Equally, don't use your dowsing as a substitute for common sense. In France you can often see some little man in a café twiddling a pendulum over his cup of coffee to see if, having bought it, it's still safe to drink; and in one of London's better-known bookshops I've often seen a woman waggling a pendulum over a pile of books, trying to get it to tell her which ones to buy. Now this is just plain daft! If you haven't got the wit to solve those 'problems' on your own, you shouldn't be using a pendulum anyway.

A matter of responsibility

Once you start serious work in dowsing, you'll soon find that all the 'objects' you deal with appear to have minds of their own. All of them – people, plants, minerals, metals, stones, places on, above and below the ground, even concepts and ideas – in their role as images in dowsing can be awkward, cantankerous, unreliable, even treacherous; as images they all have a sense of mind and purpose. Not necessarily 'mind' in the usual sense of the word, in fact rarely so, but since they all exist as ideas and images in the mind, they can all act as at least semi-independent entities within it. Since in dowsing you're operating in the mental world, the world of the mind, you have to observe and be responsive to their reactions and needs if you're going to get reliable results from them.

If that sounds a rather esoteric notion, which it probably does, then it can be put in one plain, ordinary word: *responsibility*.

To analogize, it's becoming patently obvious that we aren't being responsible in and to the physical world. The materialistic notion of 'Man's increasing control over the blind forces of nature' is assumed to be a one-way process – for how *could* nature possibly control the great god Man? We've only been able to call that black comedy of irresponsibility 'progress' because its real results have been so long a-coming – so long a-coming that we've kidded ourselves that they've quietly disappeared, like dust swept under a carpet. But it's not a one-way process, it's a multiple-level interaction system, and every action within a closed interactive system has to cause a reaction somewhere (and somewhen) in that system. And that's becoming rather clear nowadays, isn't it?

In dowsing you're working with the same interactive system, but at a higher level: the results of any mistakes come fast and hard – the higher the level of operation, the faster and harder – and often by unlikely and unexpected routes. You are directly responsible, in both senses of the word, for what you do or fail to do in this: you can't pass the buck to anyone else. So mistakes can be expensive – and not only financially, since in some areas there is a risk of damaging yourself and others mentally, physically and otherwise. More about that in Chapters 12 and 13.

This isn't meant to be a 'scare story', or anything equally stupid: the point of this is, simply, experiment by all means, but be aware of what you're doing. Before tackling anything, particularly in high-level work, wait until you have at least *some* idea of what you're doing and what forces you're dealing with – for while it's easy enough to get into trouble, it's not so easy to get out of it. And practice first before trying anything in which it will matter if you make a mistake. . . .

A matter of profit In many cases it's perfectly reasonable to ask for expenses or a fee if someone employs you for a dowsing job, and even, in the case of a dowser skilled enough to make a profession of it, to live on those fees. But there's a strange built-in catch here: if you push it too far, your results will start to go subtly but expensively wrong. This isn't so much a rule as an empirical fact – in the long term you cannot make and keep a large profit through dowsing. A quiet living, yes; a fortune, no. There are various reasons I can think of for this: your mind becomes stuck on the abstract idea of 'profit', thus jamming any other qualitative sample; you start 'trying' instead of letting the answers arise by themselves; you start getting bored – but I suspect it goes deeper than that, *through* those reasons and the 'matter of responsibility', to something akin to the Hindu concept of *karma*.

This is true not only of money, but of *all* facets of an inflated ego, facets such as pride, self-importance and arrogance, dogmatism, credulity and incredulity, and the rest of the 'seven deadly sins'. Unless it's kept well under control, the ego can take an awful hammering in dowsing, constantly being fooled and made to look a fool. In this game, the only way out of that hammering is to be humble . . . and sceptical.

A matter of necessity This is a 'matter' which ties the other three together, and leads them and you straight into the tangled realms of the Old Magic. The point here is that, as is also implied by traditional magical experience and modern paraphysical research, *dowsing will tend to work according to need – not will.* But don't ask me what determines need. . . .

The more you *need* the results the more reliable they will be, and conversely, the less you need them – the more you are just trying to 'prove a point', or are merely playing about – the less reliable they will be. I haven't the faintest idea *why* or *how* this should be so – it's just another empirical fact. If you don't need the results, 'something' tends to jam the reception of them – a process that can only be felt intuitively rather than recognized intellectually. But whatever this 'something' is, its effect increases with increasing level of operation; it seems to act as the 'feedback' mechanism in the 'matter of responsibility'; and it seems to be the same 'something' as that which demands humility in the 'matter of profit'. It's important to realize that your intentions play a crucial rôle in the reliability of the results; and therefore you must be sure of your intent, be aware of *why* you are operating, before you start any operation.

If things start to go wrong when I'm trying to dowse, I have a favourite expletive : *meng.* It's the name of the fourth hexagram of the *I Ching,* and means 'youthful folly'. . . .

Safety mechanisms All these 'matters' and processes act as safety mechanisms, protecting that massive interaction system – and you – against the effects of your mistakes, acting as cut-outs on your operations to prevent the system from having to blow its equivalent of a fuse. Use your intuition as your own protection while you're working: listen to the 'sounds that are no sounds', trust your sense of the 'feel' of the operation. If you feel that something seems wrong, and that your instrument is reacting a little strangely, *stop*. Leave it till another time, another place. Most times it won't matter; it's only those cut-outs coming into effect, and that's what they're there for. But note that the danger (or, rather, lack of safety) induced by disregarding these intuitive warnings and carrying on, increases with the level of the operation: if, as in some of the techniques described in Chapters 12 and 13, you are catalyzing changes in some of the basic forces of the interaction system, and make a serious mistake, the system may have no option but to blow a 'fuse' immediately. If you're not experienced enough to know how to protect yourself in this kind of work, the fuse it blows may be you.

For the same reason *never* use basic dowsing for very high-level work like ghost-hunting (true ghosts, that is – not the 'stored-image' type which Tom Lethbridge describes in his books and which is relatively harmless). I've done that just once, working under a friend's direction. I held up a pair of rods, started walking across the room, and we had a poltergeist starting within five seconds flat. If my friend hadn't had a lot of experience in handling that kind of problem, the end result could have been decidedly nasty, so it's not an experiment I intend to repeat.

If you note the various precautions and problems described above and in Chapters 2, 4 and 9, and keep them vaguely in mind while you're working, you won't need to worry about them. The problems shouldn't arise, and so neither should their inherent risks. In a controlled situation the risks are so small as to be irrelevant; but in an uncontrolled situation, with arrogance, ignorance and plain stupidity given free rein, the dangers are very real indeed. So if, despite these warnings, you're going to take a 'devil-may-care' attitude in this kind of work, just *do* be careful. . . .

But that's enough of these esoteric and metaphysical statements – on to practical applications.

11 Prospection and analysis

I haven't the space in this book to describe all the applications in detail – like the techniques section, this chapter and the two that follow are intended only to whet your appetite and give you a starting point for your own ideas. To help you in that, there is also an appendix on page 154 which includes a list of books and organizations which can tell you more about particular aspects of dowsing. With them you should be able to carry on where this book has to leave off.

In this chapter I'll be covering some of the more common applications, most of them dealing with concrete problems that have tangible results – though some aspects deal with abstract problems whose 'solutions' may well be intangible and impossible to prove. But to start with, a nice mundane problem: tracing a leak in a water pipe.

Tracing a leak First, the obvious point: find the pipe. If you don't know where it is, use the usual positional and directional techniques (on- or off-site), keeping the idea or the image of the pipe clearly in mind. Once you've found the pipe, follow its course using a tracking technique. If you do know where one or both ends are – at the stopcock or the house, for instance – start from an end that you know and use a tracking technique to follow its course, as above. In both cases, while you're doing this, keep in mind that you're looking for a leak, some kind of discontinuity or change from the normal condition of the pipe or flow, the idea being that as you cross the point of the leak, the instrument's reaction should change from a tracking one to a positional one. Mark that point. Now use a depthing technique to find the depth of the *leak* (not the pipe – that's important as a check). Even if you do know that the pipe is only a couple of feet down, it's still worth depthing anyway, for the 'leak' may not be a leak at all, but something else further down. A quick check of the depth will clear that for you – it's just something to watch out for, one of the catches.

Catches   That catch above can be lessened by using angle rods, since they have different reactions for something *on* the line and something *crossing* the apparent line. Other instruments can't tell the difference. It's also important to check and double-check your results – though a word of warning here: if you endlessly check and recheck your results, you'll start to get nonsense reactions, as though the instrument or the problem is tired of answering the same old question. *Meng!*

Another catch is that there may be more than one leak. Go over the whole length of the pipe to see if there are any more leaks in it – never assume there will only be one. While you're doing that, beware of jumping to 'obvious' conclusions about the course of the pipe – sometimes they take the craziest of courses, as in Fig. 54. This was at a country house in Scotland. I think the pipe must have been laid simultaneously by two gangs of workmen, one inside and one outside the high garden wall, each with a different idea as to where the pipe was supposed to be going! Not only that, they had also laid it alongside a hedge whose roots (not surprisingly) had over the years riddled the pipe with holes – so much so that it couldn't be repaired. Ah well, such is life!

Blockages and breakages   These are dealt with in the same way, the only difference being that while tracking you should be looking for a different kind of discontinuity – by blockage, by breakage, or whatever – and keeping that idea in mind. But do remember that *finding* the discontinuity isn't the same as *mending* it – you've still got to dig a hole to mend the thing . . . which is your only proof, too.

Water divining   Water divining, in the sense of looking for new water supplies, is in practice little different from tracing a leak – only this time

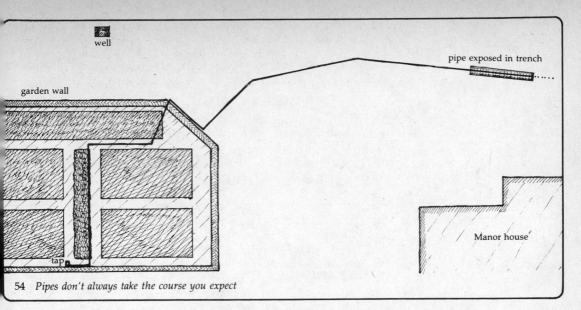

well

garden wall

pipe exposed in trench

Manor house

tap

54 *Pipes don't always take the course you expect*

you're trying to make a leak, not mend one! But it's not some-thing to take on casually, for a number of reasons. The first is one of cost – if you make a mistake in tracing a leak, you'll only have lost the little time and effort it takes to dig a small hole, but well-digging is a costly business. Even a shallow well may cost hundreds of pounds, while a deep one may cost tens of thousands – so mistakes can be mighty expensive, especially if you're the one who has to foot the bill.

Another problem: in Britain the present water-supply system uses almost all the water that's accessible, so you'll either have the expense of drilling deep, or the temptation to divert some-one else's supply (which is both unethical and illegal). You'll have to be both lucky and very sure of your skill – in knowing where the water is coming from and going to – to be able to by-pass that problem. But in many other countries, particularly in the 'Third World', this is anything but a problem – there's an urgent need for water and usually plenty of it relatively acces-sible, assuming you know how to find it and can raise enough money to hire or make a small drilling rig. 'Intermediate technology' buffs please note!

But back to water divining itself. As I mentioned a moment ago, it's basically the same as tracing a leak:

'I would hold up my rods, and they should swing to the nearest point of the stream to me. Then I would follow the line of the rods until I get over the stream. Once there, if I say to myself "Which way is the stream flowing?", the rods should point to the downflow of the stream, and I can then follow its course either upstream or downstream'.

That's how one friend puts it, anyway. Simple enough, though you can in fact make it even simpler. Although the problem is made up of a number of sub-problems – What kind or quality of water? Within what maximum depth? Within what area on the surface? How much water? and so on – you often don't need to break it down into those sub-problems, to be handled separately by the various qualitative, quantitative, positional and directional techniques. Instead, you can combine all the sub-problems into a compound mental sample – something like 'I'm looking for a water-bearing fissure carrying at least 1000 gallons per day of retrievable water of drinkable quality, no more than 100 feet down, and I'd like my instrument to react if and when there is one directly beneath my feet.' Frame that question, that compound mental sample, in your mind as clearly and precisely as you can – you know by now that that's important.

Note that an easy snag to get caught on here is to say to yourself 'I'm looking for water . . .' because it's unusual in Britain to find a place where there *isn't* any water below ground. Apart from the local water-table – which in fact you probably won't even register on your instruments, since you and they will tend to react to change, movement, discontinuity, rather than the smooth 'background noise' that the table represents – there are all the little surface and sub-surface trickles of water left over from last week's rain, all of which will confuse you if you let them. These are usually no use to you at all – what you want to find are the narrow water-bearing fissures, or fissure-like flows, which often run through even the driest of areas, fissures whose position even an expert geologist can only guess, and which you should *know*. These fissures are often more valuable as a water supply than the water-table, for since the level of the water-table tends to go up and down like a yo-yo according to the season, wells relying on it tend to dry up suddenly in a bad season. But the fissures remain relatively fixed in place and depth, and in many cases their flows vary but little with the season – though it is important to do some time dowsing to check, and to estimate the probable variation. I'm told that it's not all that unusual to find two wells side by side on a farm – one, perhaps as much as a couple of hundred feet deep, quite dry, and the other, a few feet away and a mere twenty or thirty feet deep, full almost to the brim with clear water. But you will need to fix and mark the fissure's position-relative-to-the-surface as precisely as you can, for they are often no more than a few inches across.

A typical site for a well will be at a 'knot' or intersection of water-lines such as described at the end of Chapter 7, though perhaps it might be easier to find a site by using a mental sample like 'Where is the best site in this area for a well?' But the best advice I can give you in this is to go and ask a professional water-diviner to help you – there are still quite a few around, and most of those who are members of the British Society of Dowsers will be only too glad to help.

Catches Plenty of catches! For a start, you've got all the catches of tracing a leak to contend with – check your results, watch that you're not jumping to conclusions, note that there may be a better site elsewhere in the area, and all the others. And now for some more. . . . A simple one first: note that the Bishop's Rule that I gave as an elementary depthing rule tends to be confusing on sloping ground – for what *precisely* is meant by 'the distance out'? If you use the Rule on a slope (according to the semi-physical system of dowsing), you're supposed to make allowances for the angle of the slope – but I for one don't enjoy doing complex trigonometrical calculations on a wet and windy hillside! I suggest that you ignore the angle of the slope or, better still, double-check using two different techniques. Note also that, as in the positional part of tracing a leak, the first depth you come to may not be the 'true' one. There may be several apparent depths (often known as 'sidebands' from the reaction they cause in the Bishop's Rule), and you've got to find the right one. You've also got to watch out for complete 'ghost images' rather like the 'virtual' images of conventional optics, which may be displaced both in depth and apparent position-relative to-the-surface from the 'true' image. One way of checking this is to survey two or three times, at different times of the day, for these 'ghosts' tend to move about a bit – but beware, for this isn't always the case. If you don't watch out for them, they can throw your estimates out expensively. So get someone else to check for them too, if you can. Get that someone to check all your results.

There's always a nasty moment if nothing happens when the drill reaches the estimated depth. Assuming that you're sure of both the estimated position and depth (if you're not, you shouldn't be drilling!), you've then got two options, though one of them is very much a last resort. The first is to keep drilling to at least ten per cent further than your original estimate – certain kinds of rock can alter the apparent depth for some dowsers, among other things. If that doesn't produce any water, check the position and drilling angle of the rig, for in many kinds of rock if the bore misses the fissure by only a few inches – let alone a few feet – the water won't be able to break through. If this does seem to be the case, it's time for that second option, that of enlarging the bore at the estimated depth of the fissure – a small charge of dynamite will often work wonders! But if *that* doesn't work, you'd better think of something else, and fast. . . .

So I repeat: if you want to take up water-divining seriously *see a professional* – he's got the experience. What I've told you here may be misleading, because what works well enough for me may not work for you at all. You need to learn and practise on techniques tailored to your needs and abilities, and for that there's no better way than the old master-apprentice system.

Mineral dowsing You can dowse for any kind of mineral in the same way as water-divining, using physical samples, or a list of minerals, or just a clear visualization as a mental sample. If nothing else, it's a pleasant and simple way of building a collection of minerals.

If you intend to dowse for the extraction of some mineral on a commercial scale, there are a number of extra points to watch. You have to establish not only the *presence* of the mineral, but also its *concentration* at any particular point and the *shape* and *size* of the seam. Be as precise as possible – don't generalize. To give an example, at the time of the first North Sea oil surveys a number of wild generalizations were made, stating that the oil-fields extended for hundreds of square miles. Which they do, of course, but what was needed was the sizes and positions of the individual pockets of oil and gas within the fields – and these are much smaller, extending a few square miles at most. It's no use telling a rig crew the general area of the field: they need to know the precise position of a pocket, to know exactly where to start their bore, for the drill has to hit that pocket right in the middle. As I said before, *be precise*.

But while you have to keep the economics of commercial extraction in mind, it's also important to consider what might be called the ethics of what you're doing. Our ability to damage the ecology of this planet – to indulge in a dangerous form of rape, if you like – is increasing at a frightening rate, and it seems that increasing destructive ability is paralleled by an increasing irresponsibility. We are of necessity parasites on this planet, and, as our own parasites have to do with us, we must be careful not to poison our 'host' till it dies or is forced to take its equivalent of an antibiotic. So are you sure that what you're doing is necessary, in an ecological sense? If not, be careful – for there's something moving at the present time, something 'in the air', which seems to imply that that part of the 'matter of necessity' is about to make a savage comeback. . . .

Analysis This kind of work is best handled by the 'Yes'/'No'/'Wrong question' system with the pendulum, as described in the last chapter. The advantage of dowsing in, say, chemical analysis is that it can be used as a non-destructive test – you don't have to remove or physically *do* anything to the sample you're trying to analyse. A disadvantage is that it isn't always reliable, of course, but never mind!

I'll take that example of chemical analysis a little further. First, ask yourself or the pendulum – or however else you operate – if the sample in front of you is a single substance or a mixture. Keep your mind on the job – don't get led astray trying to analyse the composition of the glass jar or the stains on it. Anyway, if it's a single substance, go to the next paragraph! If it's a mixture, you've first to find how many substances there are, and then fix your mind on just one of them, to make it the temporary 'sole substance for analysis'.

Start with general questions, questions about the general class of the substance, and so move steadily towards more and more specific ones. For instance, start by asking if the substance is organic or inorganic. If it's inorganic your task is relatively easy, for if I remember my schoolboy chemistry correctly, there are only a few thousand inorganic compounds compared to several hundred thousand organic ones.

So inorganic ones first. Is it an element or a compound? If it's an element, run through the list of elements till you find the right one. If it's a compound, work your way through the list of elements again looking for the constituent elements, and also their proportions in the compound. You'll have to go through the list several times, but try to get the first element of the chemical formula first, then the second, then the third, and so on. If the proportions tie in to give a recognizable chemical formula, *don't* assume that it must be right. *Always check it back against the sample in front of you* – ask something like 'Is this the right chemical formula?' If it is right, well and good; if not, start again, thankful not to have made a stupid blunder!

If the sequence of elements and proportions don't give a recognizable formula, you'll have to go through a list of the compounds of those elements, looking for one which gives a reaction on the bob – though beware, for there may be several possible compounds. Another way of doing this is to see if the compound is one of any recognizable class, such as an acid, an alkali, an alcohol, an ester, or some recognizable salt such as a carbonate, a sulphate, a sulphite, a silicate or any other. Having found the 'tail-end' class, try and tag a front-end to it and to the formula – for instance, if the front-end of a sulphate is iron, giving either ferrous or ferric sulphate, it's quite easy to find the final formula from there. But remember, once you have what appears to be the final formula, *always check it back*.

Organic analysis is done in the same way, though it's made more difficult by the sheer number of possible organic compounds. But again, try to establish the elements and their respective proportions; again try and break it down into sub-classes – acids, alcohols, amines, aliphatics, aromatics, and so on. Just see what you come up with.

But if you already know that the three colourless liquids in front of you are solutions of sugar, salt and weedkiller, those respective labels are quite good enough to separate them – you don't need to go to all the bother of establishing their chemical structures! So use the simplest possible labels in your analysis – complications not only complicate the issue, but also increase the probability of mistakes.

Catches The worst of these is that it's all too easy to jump to an 'obvious' conclusion as to what the substance is. As usual, the reliability of any experiment will depend on the experience and the degree of subjective control of the operator – under poor conditions an 'analysis' will be reduced to the level of guesswork. But a skilled operator should be able to produce little short of perfect accuracy in normal working conditions, especially on simple two- or three-way decisions like the one in the last paragraph. The more complicated the analysis, the greater the possibility of mistakes, of course. If you happen to be a school sciences teacher, you could find this kind of experiment a useful demonstration for your pupils of the problem of subjectivity and objectivity in science. Since the reliability depends entirely on the observer, try them out on that three-way experiment, to see how close they can get to the ideal of 'the observer, in observing, plays no part in the observation'.

Lost and found This is a loose classification for the extension into practice of those 'parlour tricks' that I hope you tried at the beginning of the last chapter. The idea is to use dowsing techniques to find any 'object' that you need. For the definition of 'object' look into your mind – an 'object' can be an old coin, your keys, the dog next door, your husband or wife, anything. But there's the usual catch: anything you *need*, not necessarily everything you *want*. Beware!

People An anecdote should give you an idea of what can be done. Another friend of mine had to contact a colleague urgently – which would have been simple enough had the colleague not been quite so nomadic. My friend phoned the two numbers he had – 'He hasn't been here for months' and 'Sorry, he left with all his stuff a couple of hours ago'. So he took a pendulum and the *A to Z* atlas of London, and started on the index map. The pendulum clearly indicated one page, and then one street on that page . . . that's better. What kind of a place? A hotel. But which hotel? He hunted out a trade directory, and on the list of hotels for that street the pendulum reacted once. Is that the right hotel? Yes. So he phoned the hotel and asked if his colleague was there. 'No, sir, no-one of that name here.' But something nagged at him intuitively, and he left a message there, 'just in case'.

Two hours later his colleague rang him from that hotel, somewhat perplexed, and asked how did he find him, because he'd only decided to go there an hour ago?

Now that's an extreme example, but it should give you the general idea. The story *is* true, by the way. Remember that the information you can get from this kind of work is *only* information – untested and unreliable information, not fact. By all means use that information, 'on the off-chance', to see if it *is* true, but *never trust it*. The 'matter of necessity' operates a lot here, as I implied earlier: if it isn't necessary for you to find that person, you'll probably find yourself being led on a right old wild goose chase . . . and that's happened to me more than once.

Animals One of the commoner problems a dowser is asked to deal with is finding a lost pet. There are at least two ways of doing this. The first is to play at bloodhound and get hold of some object that can be used as a sample of the animal – a strand of hair, its blanket, its drinking bowl, a photograph or something like that – for use in the usual on- or off-site positional and directional techniques. A second method is to work on a map, starting from the point where the animal was last seen, and track on the map its movements from that time and place. Use an ordinary sample as above, or else try to build up a mental image of the animal by getting the owner to describe its shape, size, colour and other characteristics – get the owner to build up an image of the animal in his or her mind for you to use. But invent and use other ways of handling this problem as you like – one more way would be to ask a series of directional mental questions.

But you aren't restricted to chasing recalcitrant pets. One of my students was particularly fond of wild deer (studying, not eating!) and used dowsing techniques to locate and track the Richmond Park herd. He used to start at home on a large-scale map of the Park, getting first the present position of the herd on the map, then the speed and direction in which they were moving, so as to get an idea of where they were likely to be when he got there. Once there, he used a scan directional technique to locate their new position, and incidentally to check his map dowsing. He was usually right.

In this case he used photographs of the deer as his samples, sometimes using a photograph as a sample for a specific animal, sometimes the same photograph as a sample for deer in general. The important thing, he said, was to frame in his mind the context in which he was using the sample – something for you to bear in mind.

Objects First, and most important, decide precisely what object it is that you're looking for – you can't really do anything till you've done that. Then either use a physical sample of that object, stating in your mind the context in which you're using it, or else frame the idea of the object in your mind as clearly as you can, holding it there as a sample while you're working. And carry on from there, using whatever techniques you feel might be suitable – I hope I've given you enough examples by now! But while you're working, keep your intuition wide open; use it to help you interpret what's going on. Sometimes, when I can't find some object, it seems clear that it's just being awkward and playing 'hard to get'; but at other times there's a distinct feeling, an intuition, that something is 'jamming' the operation. The 'jamming' mechanism is usually the 'matter of necessity', or one of the other 'matters' – but it's useful to know that that is what has gone 'wrong', so keep your intuition wide and alert.

Abstract objects and ideas As I implied at the beginning of this chapter, you aren't limited to looking for things tangible – you can also look for things intangible, ideas, concepts and so on, things ranging from microwave radio transmission paths (which, though physical, happen to be outside the normal range of the senses) to abstract ideas like 'Where is the best place to plant this sapling?' The former problem is a routine piece of positional work – although literally 'extra-sensory perception' – but with one interesting change: when looking for a path's position-relative-to-the-surface, you have to bear in mind that the path itself is *above* ground, not below it. You won't have much luck looking for one underground if it isn't there, will you?

Thinking about the 'sapling' problem, it's difficult to work out just how problems like that are handled in dowsing. I've never been able to decide whether the instrument's reaction is in answer to an intuitive multiple-factor question – the factors in this case including water supply, available sunlight, shelter, competing and companion plants, type and fertility of soil, all in relation to the ongoing conditions – or to a simple idea of 'resonance' or 'harmony' with the local surroundings. Perhaps it comes to the same thing in the end – I don't know – but anyway it's something I will be looking at more closely in the next chapter.

Do remember that while working on tangible objects you're simply using dowsing techniques as a sort of 'back-up' or extension to your normal senses, whereas with intangible objects you're actually *overriding* those senses, and operating at a higher level. Consequently in working with intangible objects the old problem of subjectivity becomes absolutely critical – it *must* be controlled before reliable results can be achieved.

12 Agriculture and medicine

In reading this chapter I hope you will realize that this can only be a limited introduction to the field – for if there's one aspect of dowsing in which it's essential to know *exactly* what you're doing, it's medical work. Agricultural dowsing isn't quite so fussy, fortunately – animals and plants seem to be able to shrug off the dowser's blunders without much injury or complaint.

A note on terminology

There's some confusion over two terms in dowsing literature. The word *radiesthesia* is still used in its original sense of 'sensation of radiation' (whatever that's supposed to mean), but is mostly used to mean 'medical dowsing'. *Radionics,* the specific form of medical dowsing which uses as its instrument a 'box' containing a number of dials in a particular sequence or pattern, seems to be a compound-word formed from 'radiesthetic electronics' – so the word is another product of the tangle over the assumed physical basis of dowsing.

'Harmony'

One of the key concepts in dowsing for agriculture and medicine is the one of 'harmony' that I mentioned briefly at the end of the last chapter. The example I gave there was 'Where is the best place to plant a tree?', which in effect is asking 'Where would this tree be most in harmony with me, the soil, the surrounding plants and the whole of the interaction-system of nature?' This idea extends on into veterinary and human medicine, dealing with both the 'internal harmony' of bodies and their 'external harmony', their relationship with the 'outside world'.

'Alimentary radiesthesia'

An easy introduction to this concept of harmony is Henry de

France's 'alimentary radiesthesia', about which, in its overdone form, I was rather rude when talking about the 'matter of level'. Providing you use it for interest and experiment only, it's fine – it's when you build waggling a pendulum over your coffee into an obsession that it becomes a dangerous bore.

The idea is to test the food on your plate, or the drink in front of you, to see if it is 'harmonious with you', 'good for you'. Use the usual 'Yes'/'No' system for this. If the pendulum says 'No' – which it probably will – you've then got to find out why. Is there too much food there, or too much drink? Is one particular part of the meal wrong? Is it overcooked? Is it lacking something? It's a good way of learning about nutrition, I suppose – but play with it, don't take it too seriously, or you may find yourself either too worried to eat anything at all, or else merrily munching cyanide (or something equally ridiculous) because the pendulum's told you it's delicious. . . . Be realistic!

Diagnosis   Otherwise known as analysis of a problem, so you can see that it's handled in the same way as the chemical analysis of the last chapter. The analytical technique is much the same for *any* form of analysis – the only thing that changes is the list of possibilities. Note that unlike a simple chemical analysis, you have to do a three-way analysis for agricultural and medical diagnosis: not only do you have to find whatever it is that's inefficient or damaged, but you also have to find if there is an excess of something that shouldn't be there, or a deficiency of something that should.

Agriculture   So in agricultural analysis check the soil – or the plants or animals – to see if there is any disease or toxin present, or if there is a serious excess or deficiency of some trace element. This is a simple way for farmers and smallholders to keep a check on their crops and stock, especially if done regularly. It would be a good idea to check first to see if there is any serious 'disharmony' on the farm or holding, and then to move on to any specific problems from there. This would save a lengthy and probably unnecessary analysis each day. Just try it for yourself in practice.

Companion plants   Taking this idea of harmony a little further, you should be able to find which plants go well together and fend off each other's pests – and equally which ones hate each other. The Soil Association (Walnut Tree Manor, Haughley, Stowmarket, Suffolk) have done a lot of work on this, though whether dowsing was used in the research I don't know. Use the mental-question system to compare plants or seeds, or even descriptions of the plants in a seed-merchant's catalogue. Another way some dowsers use is to hold a pendulum between the two types of plant and note whether the pendulum oscillates or gyrates. You'll have to find which means what for you though, since (as usual) it varies from person to person.

Medicine   That three-way test for the presence of damage or disease and for the presence or absence of specific substances is valuable in both human and veterinary medicine, because human patients tend to give very woolly descriptions of their problems, and because animal patients can't tell the doctor anything anyway. Conventional diagnosis is often reduced to the level of an intelligent and observant guess. Even then, that guess can be thrown way out by the problem that the cause of the symptoms the patient shows may be itself an effect of another problem. To give an analogy, if you pull downwards on your collar you'll feel pressure at the back of your neck; the site of the pressure, or 'pain', isn't the same as that of the pull, or 'disease', and forcibly relieving the pressure at the back of the neck (analogous to the conventional medical approach of treating the symptoms) will only shift the pressure somewhere else. Analytical dowsing, used as an adjunct to conventional diagnosis (but *not* as a substitute for it) can help to find the primary cause of the problem and where it is hiding. An interesting point that comes up in diagnosis is that you can dowse for the preconditions of an illness, locating a problem *before* it shows up as physical symptoms, so dowsing can be used in preventative as well as curative medicine. This is one of the most valuable uses of medical dowsing – for surely prevention is better than cure?

The diagnosis can be done using lists of organs as reference points against which to test for diseases and the like, but as with

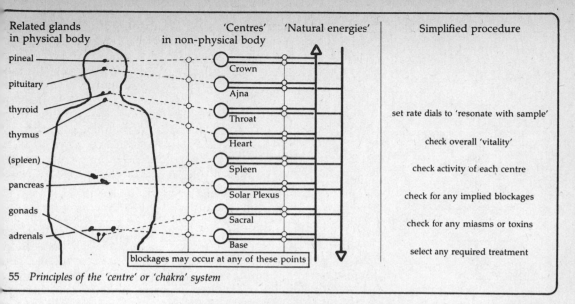

Related glands in physical body	'Centres' in non-physical body	'Natural energies'	Simplified procedure
pineal	Crown		
pituitary	Ajna		
thyroid	Throat		set rate dials to 'resonate with sample'
thymus	Heart		check overall 'vitality'
(spleen)	Spleen		check activity of each centre
pancreas	Solar Plexus		check for any implied blockages
gonads	Sacral		check for any miasms or toxins
adrenals	Base		select any required treatment

blockages may occur at any of these points

55   *Principles of the 'centre' or 'chakra' system*

the other physically-based systems this tends to get increasingly complex and confusing the deeper you go into it. So to simplify this tangle, several multiple-level systems have recently been developed. One of these is David Tansley's 'centre-' or 'chakra-based' system, which I mentioned briefly in Chapter 5. This assesses the levels of activity and efficiency of eight non-physical 'centres' and checks for any toxins or 'miasms' acting on any or all of those centres. The whole system thus needs to handle diagnostically only two or three dozen variables, compared to the several thousand needed in the older radionic systems, and its reduced complexity is usually more efficient and reliable.

'Vitality'   The levels of activity and efficiency of the individual centres in that system combine to give an overall level, a level of the 'vitality' of the body and mind of the patient. It's a good idea to use this as a routine check before going on to do a full diagnosis, whatever system you're going to use. Test it with any sample of the patient and, using the idea of a 'percentage of vitality', count

127

the number of rotations of a pendulum (use a fixed scale of te: or a hundred), or else turn a dial marked with a scale of ten or hundred until the point where a pendulum reacts. The techni que's the same whether the patient happens to be a person, cow, a cat, a cabbage or a turnip; both methods should give yo the effective percentage of an ideal level of vitality at the time c diagnosis.

Meddling You can decide from that level of vitality whether the patien needs looking at more closely. But remember that very few things do work with perfect efficiency – it's only if the level i seriously low, taking into account factors like the age of th patient, that anything further needs to be done. If things ar ticking over fairly well, regardless of what you might seem t find by nosing further into the state of the patient, *leave it alone* If you keep meddling and interfering, the only result will be tha you'll make things worse.

But of course this is one of the inherent problems of all 'fringe medicine – it's all too easy for it to become a hypochondriac' heaven. So two points always to bear in mind are check you results wherever possible against other methods of diagnosis including the more conventional ones; and never intrude o anyone's state of health unless it's absolutely clear that some thing does need doing. I repeat – *don't meddle*!

Treatment There are many different kinds of treatment, all of them usefu for some purposes, and none of them – as far as I can see - usable for *all* purposes. Quite apart from the variations on th conventional themes, I know of one book on fringe medicin which lists about sixty different systems, and I know that th author left some out. You don't have to know all of them - though if you're going to use one you need to know it well – bu from a practical point of view it's useful to know enough abou the basic principles of the major systems to know when to refe a patient to a practitioner in any particular field. You'll find tha in a dowsing diagnosis you should be able to find not only th root of the patient's problem, but also the most suitable systen of treatment, and often the specific solution to the patient' problem within that system.

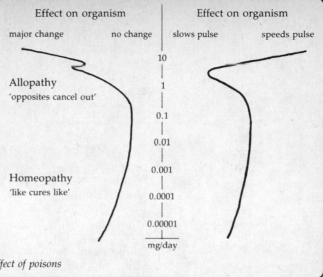

Many poisons work paradoxically, in that at certain dosages they may produce one effect, while at higher dosages (or as the subject's sensitivity changes over a period of time) they may produce exactly the opposite effect. Barbiturates are a classic example of this: at low dosages they act as sedatives, while an overdose may kill the subject not by over-sedation, but by over-stimulation.

The two graphs show the relative effects of a range of doses of digitalis for a typical subject.

Note: effective dosages vary greatly from patient to patient – these graphs should be regarded as diagrammatic only, showing principles rather than precise effects.

Effect on organism

major change   no change

Allopathy
'opposites cancel out'

Homeopathy
'like cures like'

Effect on organism

slows pulse   speeds pulse

10
1
0.1
0.01
0.001
0.0001
0.00001
mg/day

56   *Homeopathy, allopathy and the paradoxical effect of poisons*

Homeopathy   Homeopathy is the most common form of fringe medicine, so much so that it *is* officially recognized – you can get homeopathic treatment through the National Health Service. The two key concepts of the system are that, unlike conventional medicine, the patient is regarded and treated *as a whole* rather than as a collection of physiological and biochemical bits and pieces; and that rather than using drugs to counter the apparent symptoms (the conventional medical approach, called allopathy) the treatment will usually be a minute dose of some substance which in an allopathic-type dose would *emphasize* those symptoms – in other words, 'like cures like'.

Homeopathy and allopathy aren't opposed to each other: neither is 'wrong'. Their apparent opposition is caused by their using opposite wings of what is known as the 'paradoxical effect of poisons' – and traditional herbal medicine is parked in the middle. Some bits of homeopathic-type herbal medicine that are included in the conventional repertoire catch out many a trainee doctor – for instance, a small dose of digitalis (extracted from foxgloves) will slow the heart down, which is useful for a patient with high blood pressure. But if that dose doesn't slow the heart down enough, the one thing *not* to do is to give the patient a larger dose – *that speeds the heart up*. To increase the effect you have to *decrease* the dose. This applies not only to digitalis but to many other poisons as well – in minute doses they operate in a curative rather than a poisonous way, and are toxic only in relatively large quantities. But by 'minute doses' I do mean minute: solutions containing only a few molecules of the original substance are common in homeopathic usage, and dilutions or 'potencies' may go down as far as 10^{-400} of the original solution – known as a potency of 200^c, a dilution of 100:1 done two hundred times. In that kind of dilution there is virtually no chance that a single molecule of the original substance will be present, so I've no idea how it works – but it does.

So the idea in homeopathic diagnosis is to find the 'similimum', the substance whose allopathic effect in a healthy subject would most closely match the symptoms of the patient. This is where dowsing comes in: firstly, to check the description of the symptoms given by the patient; secondly, to find, by running down a list with a pendulum, which of the various remedies shown in the *Homeopathic Materia Medica* that roughly match that description of the symptoms is the most suitable one for that particular patient at that particular time; and thirdly, to find the correct potency and dose of that potency for that remedy and patient. Incidentally, note that high-potency remedies are just as dangerous as large doses of conventional drugs – they should never be prescribed without checking that that potency is correct and safe.

Note also that since the diagnosis relates to the condition of the patient at the time of the diagnosis only, the remedy or the course of doses of the remedy should be taken as soon as possible, for as the patient's condition changes, the remedy will go 'out of date', and may even be harmful. For the same reason, the remedy will have to be changed as the situation and the symptoms of the patient change, hopefully ending up with a healthy and stable situation. But beware – a clumsy choice of remedies and a lack of co-operation on the part of the patient can cause a 'hunting' effect, in which the patient's condition will keep changing from one problem to another without ever really getting better. And that can be anything from annoying to disturbing for both you and the patient . . . unless, of course, he or she is another wretched hypochondriac!

Again, the 'patient' can be anything – human, animal or plant. I have heard of farmers using homeopathic remedies on cattle and sheep (for apart from anything else, they're far cheaper than antibiotics, and probably do less damage in the long run) and also using homeopathic versions of fertilizers and weed- and pest-control sprays. I've often wondered how, in that case, the sprayer was cleaned out afterwards, since rinsing it out should only increase the potency of the substance . . . though I remember that the writer of the article did advise against using the same sprayer for both conventional and homeopathic sprays.

Bach remedies Bach remedies are homeopathic remedies using 'essence of flower' rather than 'essence of poison' as the active agent, and are thus supposed to be unable to do any harm, even if misprescribed. Specific flowers are steeped in water, exposed to sunlight for a few hours, and then removed. The liquid left behind is then diluted to homeopathic proportions. In all some thirty-eight flower remedies are used, including the valuable 'rescue remedy', used for emergencies. Diagnosis and prescription are much the same as for homeopathy.

Herbal medicine Traditional herbal medicine is based on some remarkably astute observations – for instance, it's only recently been recognized that the old practice of putting bread poultices on wounds and allowing them to go mouldy is a crude but effective way of applying penicillin to a wound. But being on the borderline between the two approaches, some herbal medicine is allopathic, some homeopathic, and some both (digitalis being a case in point), so extracting a usable remedy from the tangle of apparent panaceas in the old herbals is quite a job. The fact that the same herbs affect different people in different ways doesn't help either! So analytical dowsing can help a lot here: run through the list of apparently suitable herbs in your herbal, using a pendulum to pick out one or a combination that is particularly suitable for the patient and the problem you're dealing with.

Acupuncture   Human acupuncture is definitely *not* something for the amateur. The basic principle (of temporarily altering the 'flow' of a 'meridian' by inserting a fine needle at a particular point) is simple enough, but there the simplicity ends. To give you an idea, the acupuncturist has to be able to read *six* 'meridian pulses' on the wrist in addition to conventional heartbeat pulse; and since the acupuncture 'maps' you can buy are general, not specific, an unskilled person using one of them stands a fair chance of putting a needle into the wrong meridian – and that can have unfortunate results. I'm told that the acupuncture anaesthesia of inserting a needle between two toes that has recently interested conventional doctors has an awkward snag: if you put the needle in at the wrong angle, or a fraction of an inch to one side, it can induce heart failure in the patient some six months later . . . not very helpful! Dowsing can help here as a check, but I still think it's best – and safest – to have proper acupuncture training first, so that you know what you're doing.

Acupuncture of the land   But dowsing is very much involved in a form of 'acupuncture of the land' – something which I suspect is behind the old idea of 'staking a vampire at a crossroads'. The first part of this is the locating and neutralizing of 'black streams', underground streams which for unclear reasons can have a serious effect on the health of people or animals living above them: in people they can cause or catalyze anything from arthritis to polio, from migraine to major personality changes. The main clue to this is if the health of the patient markedly improves if they are moved elsewhere – even inside the same building. If this is the case, check if there is a stream or network of streams beneath the patient's bed, workspace, kitchen, or anywhere they spend a fair proportion of their time. Note that the stream may give a reaction to black, or your equivalent of it, on a Mager disc – hence the term 'black stream'.

The harmful effect of the stream can be reduced, or even neutralized, either by spraying some surface above the stream with blue paint, or in some cases by 'staking' it by hammering nails or rods into the ground above or to one side of it. Use a pendulum to check in each case the most suitable 'cure', and to find the right colour paint or the right material for the nails or rods. You can then find the best place or places to apply the cure, using standard positional techniques with any instrument. I've no idea why these unlikely-sounding stratagems should work – I only know that they do, and have been so used by farmers and farriers for centuries.

I remember once going to a small religious community in the Cotswolds. Two years before, when they had first moved in, there was no wildlife in the valley, a heavy, oppressive feeling hung over the place, and everyone staying there was affected by what seemed to be a stomach 'bug' within an hour or so of arriving. One of the community's members was, among other things, a dowser, and after a bit of probing round he came to the conclusion that some outside disturbance was affecting the overall 'balance' of the valley. So he went out with a bundle of small wooden stakes, each with a twist of copper wire at the top, and hammered one into the ground at each of the twenty places in the valley that his rod had indicated.

The effect was almost immediate. The oppressive feeling dissipated in a few days, and the sickness vanished. But even so, a year later he put another bunch of stakes (iron rod clad with copper tube, this time) in about sixty more places, and when I was there he was doing it once more, putting the finishing touches to this complex stabilization of the balance of the area. If I remember correctly, the apparent cause of the trouble was traced to a new quarry about fifty miles away – and that, of course, couldn't be dealt with directly. But this 'acupuncture of the land', to neutralize the effect of that disturbance, certainly seemed to have worked, for the birds' dawn chorus was deafening, and the valley rang with a quietness like that of a cathedral.

Faith healing   Faith healing, in the usual sense of the word, doesn't really

133

concern us here, because dowsing plays no direct part in it – though you ought to know when to refer a patient to a skilled faith healer, of course. But it does illustrate one important point: the only person who can heal a patient is that patient, so his or her attitude of mind is absolutely critical to the healing situation. Even in conventional medicine the effectiveness of any drug is known to be partly dependent on whether the patient, and the doctor before him, believes it will work. This becomes progressively more important as the level of the operation increases, from the physical level to the mental, and beyond.

The attitude of mind of the practitioner, operator, 'doctor' in fringe medicine is critically important, and not merely because of this matter of belief. You have to recognize that the patient is doing the healing, not you – all you are doing is setting up conditions favourable for healing, conditions to catalyze healing. After all, the patient's body knows itself better than his or your minds do. Another snag attached to this is that if you insist on taking an 'I'm a great healer' attitude, you can run into serious trouble, as I'll explain later.

The importance and effect of your attitude of mind can be demonstrated by experiments on plants. Take two batches of the same kind of seedlings – carrots, perhaps, or else parsley, which is notorious for its apparent dislike of dishonest persons – and put them in marked pots. Keep them apart, but otherwise as far as possible in the same environmental conditions. Each time you go past one batch, try and be friendly to the plants, talk to them, ask them how they're getting on; each time you go past the other batch, be negative to them, insult them. Then compare the rates of growth of the two batches over a few months. The de la Warr Laboratories did a number of experiments on these lines, using from a dozen to several thousand plants at a time, and with fairly consistent results. Those plants which were treated to 'positive' thoughts grew well, often surprisingly well for that kind of plant; any 'control' plants, potted at the same time as the experimental ones, grew normally; while those which were treated to 'negative' thought were often stunted or abnormally diseased. The basis of 'green fingers', perhaps?

Music and colour therapy   And just as plants react to attitudes and thoughts, so do they react to sounds and colours. Plants have been found to thrive on many kinds of classical music, but to cringe away from the impact of coarse 'pop'. Cows have been found to milk better to quiet music too, so it's reasonable to expect that people need a certain amount of quiet and 'harmonious' sounds. While music is the most obvious form of harmony, many fringe practitioners maintain that a harmony of colour is also essential for the soul, and will prescribe a dose of colour. This isn't quite as crazy as it may sound   it's quite easy, in fact. Dowsing can be used to select the most suitable type and dose of sound or colour – but here we come to an interesting point: the patient doesn't need to be present. Instead, the dose can be projected onto a sample of the patient – in other words, the treatment is 'broadcast' to the patient through the agency of the sample.

Radionic medicine   This idea of broadcasting is one of the key concepts in radionic medicine. With a sample in the sample-well of the box, the dials are turned in sequence until a number – supposedly a resonant pattern – is reached. This gives the state of a specific organ in the older-type boxes, or the state of the whole body or 'bodies' on the Tansley-type box. The emphasis on resonance and pseudo-electronic circuitry in most boxes is apparently unnecessary, since I know people who just write down on a piece of paper the numbers given by a pendulum, with the same effect; but for many people it's easier to use the clearly defined structure and system of the box. The 'matter of level' again, I suppose. But I do think that it's a mistake to assume that the box does the work, and could be left to work on the patient on its own – I am certain that without the operator's mind behind it, all the physically functionless and meaningless bits of wire and whatnot inside the box would indeed be functionless and meaningless. The box is a tuner for the operator's mind, and the mind the catalyst that gives meaning to it – the box is interdependent with the mind, not independent of it.

But to get back to practice, once a set or pattern of numbers has been reached, the next problem is to determine the most suitable type of treatment for the problem implied by those numbers. The instrument – a pendulum, or a stick-pad on the older type of boxes – can, by running through a list of systems of treatment, be used to say which system would be most suitable. Typically, the patient would be asked to take a particular homeopathic or Bach remedy – again selected from a list by the instrument – or else the remedy might be broadcast to the patient by placing the remedy and the patient's sample together for a length of time, the right time being determined by the usual quantitative techniques on the box. A broadcast remedy might be a homeopathic or Bach remedy, a sound, a colour or (among other things) a set or pattern of numbers set up on the box itself. Sometimes, particularly on the older type of boxes, the original set of numbers is reversed (by subtracting the setting on each dial from that dial's maximum reading) to give an allopathic treatment – a set of 40.448 is reversed and broadcast as 60.662 to counter *B.Typhosus Coli*, for instance – but sometimes the numbers are left the same, particularly on the later type of boxes, to operate homeopathically. Again, use your trusty pendulum to find the best technique.

Dangers The first problem in all this work is that of mis-diagnosis and mis-prescription – but here the dowser often stands a better chance of being right than his conventional counterpart. Remember to check your results against other tests whenever you can. Note that it's essential to keep your mind wide open, watching all the time for casual intrusions – jumping to conclusions – and unconscious expectations. But if you're not going to stuff the patient full of drugs, there's a useful safeguard here: since you're operating in a psychosomatic situation, patients seem to be able to shrug off many kinds of minor blunder without harm – this is particularly so with plants and animals, but less so with people.

But because you are operating directly on a psychosomatic situation, tuning directly into the multiple-level energy system of the patient, *there is a risk of feedback*, in which the patient's symptoms repeat themselves in your own body and mind, sometimes with disastrous results. This *is* an interactive system, after all. So unless you learn to know intuitively when destructive feedback is occurring, and how to block it, dump it or channel it, you can get into real trouble, especially when working on people. Unfortunately, you'll have to find your own way of defusing and diffusing this problem, since every operator has their own way of doing it – I usually 'throw it away', as though it was something collected in my hand, or else visualize it as a flow passing by me; but, as I said, you'll have to find for yourself what seems to be best for you.

The opposite side of the same coin applies if you believe that *you* are healing the patient – person, cow, cabbage, carrot or whatever it is – and not merely helping him, her or it to heal itself. By doing so *you* have to supply the patient's additional energy requirements, rather than helping the patient to find them itself – and the result of that arrogance is that a disproportionate number of fringe practitioners have died in their early forties, having effectively burnt themselves out. So please watch what you're doing!

Another point of arrogance that you need to watch is simply 'What right do you have to intrude on anyone else?' For medicine *is* an intrusion, an intrusion on the health of the patient, on the right and responsibility of the patient to look after itself. If the patient *asks* for help, that's fine – but if not, you lay yourself wide open to trouble, in a feedback sense, through your irresponsibility, and your self-righteous, self-important and simply unnecessary action. In other words, *think* before you act!

In more esoteric terms, the patient has to work out its *karma*, the reactions within the interactive system to its previous actions and inactions, and your intrusions into the apparent effects of that process of 'working out' may be a hindrance to its resolution, not a help. And that's worth bearing in mind while you're working, too.

On a more mundane level, note that treating yourself is difficult, and often impractical – it's rather like trying to lift yourself by your own bootstraps. While it's easy enough to find fault with other people, it's not so easy finding fault with yourself – since you observe through the filters of your faults, it isn't easy to see the filters themselves. Another problem arising from this is that if you aren't well sorted out yourself you can, through a kind of reverse feedback, inflict your own problems on the people you're supposed to be helping. . . .

A professional approach   I hope that from the above you now recognize that in many of the uses of medical dowsing it's essential to know precisely what you're doing – for the forces involved can do an immense amount of damage if they're allowed to get out of control. And they are often best controlled by leaving them alone. If you make a serious blunder, you can end up crippling yourself, your patients, and even 'innocent bystanders' as well. So while I have little love for élitism, I do feel that if you're going to study medical dowsing, *study it seriously, or not at all.* True, some aspects – such as the use of low-potency homeopathic remedies – are safe enough for the serious amateur to use at home or on the farm; but other areas – especially acupuncture and broadcast treatment – are not. Dabbling in this field is dangerous, so I must re-emphasize – *this is not a field for the casual amateur.*

13 Dowsing and archaeology

Or, to be more general, dowsing and the study of things relating to the past. A complete archaeology would cover a number of categories, of which only one – sometimes rudely called 'dead' archaeology – is handled by academics. This is the endless cataloguing and dating of bits of broken arrows, pottery and other assorted fragments of physical evidence, in the belief that this alone will give a complete picture of the life of the peoples of the past. Occasionally some brave department tries an experiment in social and practical archaeology (such as the Butser Farm neolithic-style farming experiment) in an attempt to see what it *felt* like, but funds are always short for this kind of 'frivolous and un-academic exercise'. Depends on your sense of values, I suppose.

Dowsing can be a help in the cataloguing game, but it's even more useful in 'live' archaeology, the study of the still-active forces – most of them non-physical – which can be shown to relate in significant ways and patterns to archaeological sites. But before going on to talk about these forces, a quick look at how dowsing can be used for conventional archaeological research.

Dowsing as a non-destructive tool Digging, the traditional archaeological research tool, has severe limitations, of which the worst is that it's a once-only affair – you can't repeat any experiment because it destroys much of its own evidence. So in recent years a lot of research has been done on non-destructive information-gathering techniques, using soil conductivity meters, metal detectors, proton magnetometers and other physical instruments. These are themselves rather limited in what they can find, and once you have enough experience as a dowser you can help a lot here. You should be able to select from the jumble of information individual classes or types of objects – bronze brooches at one point, Beaker pottery at another, the foundations of walls, post holes, cremations, anything that might be needed – using each of these labels as a mental sample. And by working first from a map, and then on-site, you should be able to help the diggers find the most profitable sites for their cuttings and trenches.

Dowsing from a time
You can also do something that can't be done by conventional means: you can directly sort out and separate the different structures – of which perhaps nothing physically remains – of the different periods of occupation of the site. If you keep in your mind the date from which you want to operate, you should only be able to find the objects and apparent structures that belong or relate to that period. By 'doing' the site several times, operating from different dates, you should be able to build up a picture of the changes in occupation and rôle of the site. But remember to hold each date carefully in your mind: if you allow yourself to drift back to real-time, you'll be back in the same tangle of information that the diggers you're supposed to be helping are trying to disentangle.

Dating
Or dowsing to a time. You should know how to do this by now – use a qualitative technique against a scale of years, decades, hundreds of years, thousands of years. You can start from any point in time – you don't have to start from real-time. When working with prehistoric material, for instance, I find it easier to work on a scale of hundreds or thousands of years BC rather than hundreds or thousands of years *ago*.

Psychometry
Psychometry can be useful in conventional archaeological work, but do remember that it is very subjective, and therefore unreliable as a 'proof' of anything. Turn back to Chapter 9 for the techniques, if you've forgotten them. If you're working with small objects, it may be easier to hold them against your forehead or your crown, or the bridge of your nose – I don't know why this works, but since it does, why bother with explanations?

Relations If you want to do any archaeological work, your relations with academics are going to be important – sure, you have something to offer them, but equally they'll have a lot to offer you. So don't go and get everybody's backs up by digging any old how and where, playing at the rapacious treasure-hunter. As I mentioned earlier, digging itself destroys much of the conventional information, so *don't do any digging without expert advice and/or direction*. If you're seriously interested in this part of the game, the best thing you can do is to go along to your local archaeological society and ask if you can dowse at their digs.

Interpretation As in other work it's essential to beware of preconceptions, and I think the safest way of doing that here is to ask the diggers to tell you what to look for – though don't let them tell you what to expect! Ask them to tell you what to look for, and then to leave you to it, since overly sceptical onlookers may well make a serious survey impossible. In many ways it's also better if you know little or nothing about conventional archaeology, but just work as a 'meter-man', an information-gatherer, working from and with the labels they give you. You should still be able to get meaningful results from those labels, even if you have no idea what they're supposed to mean – though I'd have to go into deep philosophical waters to explain why!

I think it's also best to leave any 'objective' interpretation of your information to the academics. It's possibly unkind (but, I feel, true) to say that like many other academic fields archaeology has three serious and infectious diseases. The first is an inherent dogmatism; the second is a strange inability to distinguish between information and its interpretation, between hypothesis and 'absolute truth'; and the third is a spectacular ability to miss, ignore or otherwise exclude any information that doesn't fit that observer's current theory. These diseases cripple the minds and observation of those afflicted – mind you don't catch them! The only thing that matters is what the information and the feelings derived from your dowsing mean to *you*, for it is from these that you grow.

Natural forces Social-archaeology experiments such as Butser Farm bring home the meaning of the physical forces of the weather, the sun and the seasons, but these aren't the only natural forces in this game. There are other, stranger forces beyond and behind the physical ones. Hints of these and their implications have come from a number of sources in recent years, but since this is supposed to be a book on dowsing, I'll start with Guy Underwood's 'geodetic system' – his 'pattern of the past'.

Underwood's patterns   Underwood started from the observation, which several earlier dowsers had also made, that the apparent courses of streams – water lines – tend to encircle and/or meet as 'blind springs' under barrows, standing stones and other Neolithic sites. His development of that original observation over a number of years culminated in his 'geodetic theory', which I'll go on to in a moment. But while studying the patterns made by water lines he had found other lines as well: *track lines*, which seemed to him to define the tracks and paths taken by animals and people; and *aquastats*, 'lines that are like water lines but aren't', which he never really explained. He separated the three types of line by using different grips on his 'geodetic rod', but if you want to check his work you'll probably find it easier to use verbal samples instead.

These three types of line form patterns which surround and underlie many religious and other structures and sites in significant ways. For a detailed description of this you'll need to read his *Pattern of the Past*; but, for example, water lines and aquastats will spiral in towards a standing stone; a water line or an aquastat will go almost straight up the nave of a church, leading to a 'blind spring' under the altar; in churches there is always a door or a window wherever an aquastat or track line goes through a wall; aquastats define two alternative shapes for the Uffington White Horse, one the present 'beaked' form, the other a more realistic horse. The lines twist about, rarely keeping straight for more than a few feet, and sometimes distort each other to form 'arcs', 'trivia', 'feathers', 'haloes' and several other patterns. The shapes of some of these vary according to the time of day, while the positions and shapes of others change according to a lunar timetable, major changes always occurring six

Rollright is on top of the last ridge of the Cotswolds, twenty miles north-west of Oxford, on a side road between the A34 and A44 some three miles north of Chipping Norton. The road forms part of the Oxfordshire/Warwickshire border there. The circle (known as the King's Men) is a true circle of about 100 feet in diameter, containing about 73 stones – in places it's a bit difficult to decide which bits of rock are only fragments of local stone. Most are about three feet high, with the largest just under eight feet; all are badly weather-worn. Three hundred feet away, on the north side of the road and in the next county, is the King Stone, a single stone about eight feet high, and a ruined dolmen (the Whispering Knights), a quarter of a mile to the east, completes the group. They are presumed to be Neolithic – around 2000 BC – but the site hasn't been excavated to check.

I owe many thanks to the owner, Pauline Flick, and to various of her friends and relations, for the help they gave me in my surveys there.

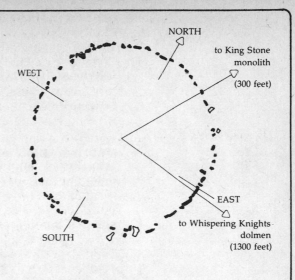

57 *Rollright: geographical layout*

This survey was done on 2nd August 1973. The various patterns are marked only where they cross the circumference of the circle – I did try tracking them individually, but soon got tangled in their interweavings and interactions.

Note how two or all three patterns may coincide, and also how they coincide with the other patterns shown on figures 59 and 60.

water line ○

track line □

aquastat △

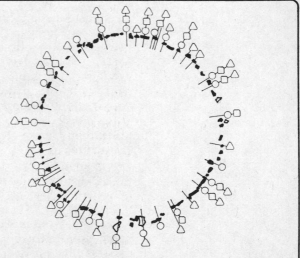

58 *Rollright: Underwood patterns at the circumference of the circle*

days after the new and full moon – a point I'd like to come back to later.

In studying the lines and 'geodetic patterns' Underwood was unable to find any variations in position other than the astronomically-linked ones, and thus assumed that the patterns were fixed and permanent. Going from this assumption and from the coincidence of the patterns with the various structures, he decided that the early architects knew that the patterns were there, thought them to be significant in religious architecture and symbolism, and therefore had deliberately used them to determine the major structure, and some minor details, of all religious and some secular sites from Neolithic times onwards, until the practice faded out with the rise of the present materialistic culture in the Reformation and the Renaissance.

If this 'geodetic theory' (or hypothesis, rather) is correct, it implies that our present architectural history will need a lot of revision. One of the reasons I started to dowse was to check this hypothesis – and I'm still working on it! This isn't the place to go into all of my work on it; but, briefly, his hypothesis, with its rigid causal connection of 'patterns determine structure' seems to be too simplistic – while the patterns do coincide with the structures to such an extent that they *can't* be chance relationships, the lines are by no means as fixed as Underwood thought, and can in fact be laid and altered quite easily. The assumption that the patterns were used *deliberately* by the old architects is also open to doubt. The connections between the builders, the structures and the patterns are much more complex than Underwood implied. Do the patterns determine the structure, or vice versa, or both, or what? They are made yet more complex by other factors and patterns which Underwood doesn't seem to have noticed. So, to give you an idea of what else to watch for, a brief look at some of these other factors.

Charges　When working on- or off-site with a pendulum from standing stones or earthworks (and many other sites or places such as altars and fonts in churches), you'll often find that your pendulum will gyrate for no apparent reason. This kind of reaction

The 'charges' shown were recorded on 2nd August 1973, by placing a hand on top of each stone in turn and noting the coincident reactions of a pendulum. '+' and '−' seem here to be equivalent to 'yang' and 'yin' respectively; some stones were found to have charges changing their polarity on a 24-second cycle, and these have been marked with an asterisk. Less than one-fifth of the stones kept the same polarity over the week of 1–7 August 1973.

The whole area of the circle was 'charged' with a number of concentric bands or 'fields', both inside and outside the circle – though only those near the circle have been shown.

rods open

rods closed

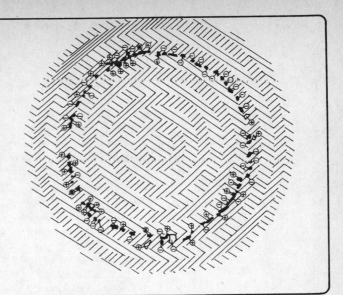

59 *Rollright: 'fields' and individual 'charges'*

Only the major internal and external connections are shown here – all are above ground. Note how the external connections coincide with groups of Underwood patterns as shown in figure 58.

The 'spin' of the circle has been clockwise every time I've tried it, though a colleague reports that he once found it to be anti-clockwise. Note how the exit points of the spin coincide with odd parts of the circle – the southern exit passes through a double line of small stones which are raised on a hump. The eastern exit of the spin, which goes towards the Hawk Stone, was powerful enough to give a helper and myself painful headaches (which took about a quarter of an hour to clear) when we accidentally triggered a pulse down the line.

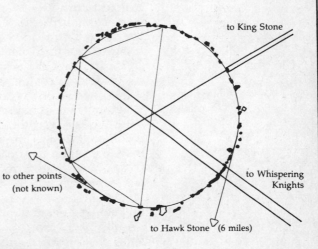

to King Stone

to other points
(not known)

to Whispering
Knights

to Hawk Stone (6 miles)

60 *Rollright: 'spin' and internal and external connections*

seems to be caused by what I call a 'charge' at that point – so called because of its resemblance to an electrostatic charge. These charges tend to change their polarity from time to time – but Christian altars are almost invariably 'positive', the only notable exceptions being many Lady Chapel altars, which are fixed at 'negative'. By polarity, or positive or negative, I mean that the point will give a 'yes'/'positive' or 'no'/'negative' reaction on the pendulum. But what these terms actually mean also seems to vary: in the case of altars it seems to be in the sense of 'yang'/'yin' or 'male-principle'/'female-principle'; at other places it seems to mean 'active/receptive' (somewhat in the sense of 'transmitting/receiving'); at others it seems to correspond to an electrostatic charge, or something very much like it; while at yet others it corresponds to 'personality', a constructive or destructive approach. I suspect that there are other forms of 'charge' as well, since it simply indicates a duality, a separation into two sides. Mental questions will tell you which type is operating.

Whole areas can be charged, too – when working at Rollright stone circle with angle rods I found that as I crossed the line of the stones the rods crossed; a few feet further they opened; a few feet further they crossed again; and so on, with seven changes in all. These alternations occurred all round the circle at the same distance from the centre, and also continued at the same rate outside the circle for at least three more changes. These alternations of charge may be similar to, or even the same as, Underwood's 'haloes'.

Directions When working at or on various places – again with a pendulum – the bob will react directionally, to mark out directions to other points with which the place is connected in some way. On a map one point may mark out forty or fifty different directions (Arbor Low stone circle is one example) which can be somewhat difficult to sort out; but fortunately most active sites have only a few of these directional connections. At Rollright four important stones operated a kind of directional 'closed shop' – stone 37 only gave a direction to stone 3, stone 3 to stone 61, 61 to 49, and 49 back to 37. It took some effort to break out of that 'circuit' and find the other directions that these stones gave.

Flow and spin   That kind of directional reaction of a pendulum may imply more than just a connection or relationship between two points, for there may also be a 'flow' component, a transfer of 'charge' between the two points in the direction shown by the bob. This flow can also be found with angle rods – when using both instruments keep the idea of 'the directional flow' as a sample in the mind. This apparent flow seems to travel *above* ground, usually in straight lines. At the circumference of stone circles (and some earthworks) the flow forms a spin, a rotation of charge, jumping from one stone to the next – clockwise in the cases of Rollright and Gors Fawr. At one point at Gors Fawr, and at two points at Rollright, the flow of the spin can leave the circle tangentially – so in a way the spin and its exit 'gates' make the circles resemble the cyclotrons that are used for research in nuclear physics.

Overground patterns   This above-ground flow of charge – whatever that might be – may travel for miles between any two connected points, forming a dead straight line only a few feet wide. One of the lines coming from Rollright travels about six miles roughly south-south-east to a stone called the Hawk Stone, and then goes off in at least two other directions from there. Other lines may be much longer – one colleague said that one he found seemed to be continuous for at least fifty miles. These are what might be called the 'external' communications of the sites; there are many other lines, including the internal directions, the flows and the spin at Rollright, which form the 'internal' and 'local' communications. This constant movement of some kind of energy from one place to another is in some ways analogous to a network of pulsed masers or lasers, each producing a low-power 'carrier' beam and occasional high-powered pulses of energy – but the *feeling* I've had when working on these overground patterns is one of working on an enormous living organism, so perhaps analogies are pointless anyway. Some of the energy-pulses seem to be astronomically linked, but others do not; and while they *can* be deliberately triggered off by a dowser, they can also be dangerous, so for safety reasons I'm not going to go into that here.

But since these 'carriers', these overground patterns, are dead straight and only a few feet wide, and do interconnect sites such as churches, barrows, standing stones, crossroads and so on, they may be the non-physical reality behind the 'ley system', the geographical alignment of ancient sites, Alfred Watkins' 'Old Straight Track'. And that's something else I want to come back to shortly! A note for ley-hunters, though: if you want to use dowsing to look for leys on-site, bear in mind that you're looking for the position-relative-to-the-surface of lines *above* ground. Use the usual positional techniques to find the line and its width and direction – if you want to find its height, which I suppose isn't all that important, try turning the Bishop's Rule upside-down.

Nodes   The intersections of these lines, and the objects and structures coincident with them, form nodes in a network of strange energies. It seems that the churches and stones are like gigantic acupuncture needles, inserted into the body of the Earth at various points as part of a massive acupuncture of the Earth itself. But it's impossible to say exactly what the relationship of site and structure is, for the sites are often active even if the structure has gone, and sometimes you can work off stones and the like even if they've been moved from their original operating site. In one case I remember, a small mark-stone had been moved a few yards from its original site (in the middle of Watling Street) to a corner of St Stephen's churchyard at St Albans. It was still active, still 'talking' to its original site, and still marking off its connections with other sites. But there does seem to be a physical component involved in this somewhere, for the limit we've so far found for the distance between a still-active stone and its original site has been a little more than half a mile.

Other nodes of energy – type unspecified – can be found at different heights on standing stones and other places such as the end-buttresses of old churches. There are usually seven of these nodes, though some smaller stones may only have the first five. The first two are usually below ground, and the third at or near ground level. The remaining four, or two on a smaller stone, can be found quite easily by running a hand up the surface of the stone, using the hand as a marker, and using a pendulum. The spacing of these nodes varies a lot from stone to stone, but the fourth and fifth will usually be within easy reach even on a very large stone, the sixth roughly half-way between fifth and seventh, and the seventh almost invariably within a few inches of the top of the stone. Dowsers John Williams and Bill Lewis found these and pointed them out to me.

The first three nodes seem to have something to do with Underwood's patterns, but exactly what and how I'm not sure. The fourth seems to be tied up with the directional flows forming the stone's local communications; the sixth handles some of the long-distance communications; but the other two are decidedly strange. In good operating conditions, if you lightly touch the level of the seventh node you'll probably feel a mild tingling sensation. For a skilled dowser this 'mild tingling' can be amplified so much that it's more like having a hefty electric shock – though without the pain! This can look as though the dowser has been thrown away by the stone, though I think it's more likely to be caused by a contraction of various back and arm muscles.

The effect triggered by the fifth node is stranger still – it seems to affect selectively the dowser's sense of balance. Put both your palms flat against the fifth-node level and lean against the stone with your arms outstretched, as if trying to push the stone over. Don't actually push! Put yourself into a dowsing frame of mind; it may also help if you tilt your head down, looking at the base of the stone. After a few seconds you'll probably feel a slight loss of balance, a falling to one side, though it may be strong enough to feel as if you're being *pushed* to one side. Don't fight it – just see what happens.

The strength of the reaction varies from person to person, and so does the direction of apparent thrust. But they both also vary to a lunar timetable – for every person I've worked with so far, the strength of the reaction is at its weakest at the time the direction of apparent thrust reverses, on the sixth day after new and full moon. And that's the same as with some of Underwood's patterns. I haven't yet been able to check if the timing of the changeover is as precise and regular (to the second) as Underwood claims it is, but I wouldn't be surprised. And there's an interesting parallel here: in the old Celtic calendar the months began on the sixth day after the new moon, each month being divided into two fortnightly periods, Anagan and Atenoux; the years began on the sixth day after the first new moon past the Spring equinox. If the patterns do alternate as regularly as Underwood claims, the changeover point would be a usefully precise point in time on which to base a calendar. But how could those 'ignorant barbarians', the Celts, possibly have known that?

Anomalies That's only one of the many anomalies within the conventional 'neo-Darwinian' view of history. Others I've found include a double date for Avebury – all the stones I tried in the outer, main circle gave a fairly conventional erection date of 2500–3000 BC on a pendulum, but the stones of the south circle and its 'cove' would only give a date of 8000–8500 BC which, I must confess, I don't really understand. Guy Underwood's *Pattern of the Past* provides more anomalous data which can be checked, as does Alfred Watkins' *Old Straight Track*; the works of John Michell and others provide parallels and coincidences that only make sense from an unconventional viewpoint; while Alexander Thom's *Megalithic Sites in Britain*, on the geometry and implied astronomy of British stone circles, has been aptly described by one professor of archaeology as 'a well constructed parcel-bomb' that puts an irreparable dent into the conventional set of assumptions about prehistory. And all these works discuss information on and possible reasons for the specific choice of certain sites for religious and secular structures – an area of information which academic archaeology conspicuously avoids.

All these unconventional sets of information are 'true', at least within their own contexts, but if you try to fit them all together into a single coherent theory that also includes the equally 'true' information from academic archaeology, you're likely to end up getting tied in impossible intellectual knots. There just doesn't seem to be any way of doing it without leaving something out. So in practice intellectualizing about history isn't worth the waste of effort it implies – it seems much more sensible to forget about trying to 'prove' anything, for what appears to be 'proof' is (as de Bono's *Second Law of Thinking* puts it) often no more than a lack of imagination, in failing to look for alternative hypotheses that would equally fit the same information. What matters far more is whether any piece of information is any *use* – whether information derived from a study of the past can be applied in a present-day situation. So use your imagination, and use information – *any* information – if and as you can, if and as you need.

14 Conclusions

As if there could be any conclusions in this game!

If you've just been reading this book to get an idea of wha
dowsing is about, now is the time to go back and start agair
reading slowly, taking your time, trying and practising the var
ous experiments, teaching yourself how to do it. Don't try t
rush it – learning any skill always takes time, although you ca
use your basic experience of that skill immediately.

But if you've been doing all the experiments, so that you'v
been collecting practical experience of dowsing while you'v
been going along, you've come to the end of everything I ca
show you here. Use this and other books as notes to refer bac
to from time to time, and in particular keep the various contro
and safeguards in mind. But apart from that, you're on you
own.

So use dowsing to help you learn to watch, to observe, to se
to listen, to feel; to help you build up and use your intuitior
Use it as a crutch for your intuition to rest on; discard it whe
your intuition no longer needs it. But use it as you like, as yo
need; use it and let it be useful; use it to be of use.

Enjoy yourself!

Appendix: Moving on

Much of this book has been necessarily vague. My aim here ha[s] been to give you enough ideas, principles and practice to enabl[e] you to build up your own approaches and techniques, rathe[r] than to give you specific but probably misleading details. Ther[e] *isn't* any *'the* way to do it' in dowsing. But in moving on, you'[ll] probably find it useful to look up other books on the subject and to find out about the various organizations in the field, so a[s] to see how other people tackle the same problems, and to us[e] their ideas and experience as stepping-stones in your ow[n] work. Below is a list of some of the books and organizations I'v[e] found useful over the years.

Books   Although a vast amount has been published in the past o[n] dowsing, there's not all that much in print at the moment - though what there is, is mostly good stuff. Many of the author[s] are proposing or defending particular theories, so remembe[r] that you will probably need to do some translation to use thei[r] ideas.

General   *Elements of Dowsing* by Henry de France, Bell, 1948 (reprinte[d] 1971). This is a lovely little book with a lot of useful ideas and [a] nice style which, despite being based on the physical system o[f] dowsing, is always easy to follow. It's also got a good chapter o[n] 'Teleradiesthesia or Superpendulism' (in other words, the mental system of dowsing) with some useful and practical explana-tions.

Ghost and Ghoul (1961), *Ghost and Divining Rod* (1963), *ESP* (1965), *A Step in the Dark* (1967), *The Monkey's Tail* (1969) and *The*

Legend of the Sons of God (1972) by T. C. Lethbridge, Routledge Kegan Paul. Tom Lethbridge is one of my favourite authors. His rambling style and brilliant observation make every one of his books a delight to read. The middle four have the most information on dowsing as such, particularly on the 'long pendulum' techniques; but all of them cover such a wide range of material, from his archaeological expeditions in the 1920s, his experiences of sailing, his experiments on dowsing, ghosts and general ESP, to his sharp asides on the state of the academic world – all subjects which bear on dowsing, even if in unexpected ways – that they really are worth going out of your way to find and read.

Radiesthesia, by Abbé Mermet, Vincent Stuart, 1959. Reprinted in paperback in 1976. While I don't much like his style, this book does contain a lot of useful information, especially on the series and serial number techniques, and on the development of the mental-questions system.

The Divining Rod, by Sir William Barrett and Theodore Besterman, republished by University Books, 1968. Originally published in England in 1926, this American reprint is available in this country. It's worth getting if you're interested in the history of dowsing, which they cover in some detail. They also cover 'scientific' tests of dowsing, biographies and activities of well-known dowsers of their time, and the general theory of dowsing – they come out in favour of a 'cryptesthetic' or multiple-level theory. Not all that much practical information, though.

The theory of dowsing from a physical and physiological point of view is covered in *The Physics of the Divining Rod* by J. C. Maby and T. B. Franklin, Bell, 1939; *Physical Principles of Radiesthesia* by J. C. Maby, privately printed 1966; and *Psychical Physics* by S. W. Tromp, Elsevier, 1949. All out of print and difficult to find. Maby and Franklin were the British Society of Dowsers' 'official researchers', and while their earlier book is clear enough, Maby's later book is not. A reprinted collection of his 'papers' (whose readability is marred by a tortuous style of writing and an appalling 'out-of-focus' quality of print), it's an excellent if depressing example of the tangle researchers get into if they try to 'explain' multiple-level phenomena – the interaction of matter, mind and beyond – with simple physical theory. Tromp's book is more useful, concerning itself with information rather than theory, and with exhaustive experiments and discussions on all the possible physical and physiological factors that could operate in dowsing. It's also got a vast bibliography – some 1496 items covering several centuries.

For the problem of psychological interference and its control, and for ideas about handling intuition, analysis and problems in general, I recommend:

The Psychology of Consciousness by Robert Ornstein, Freeman, 1972.

The Exploits of the Incomparable Mulla Nasruddin (1966) and *The Pleasantries of the Incredible Mulla Nasruddin* (1968), collections of Sufi parables edited by Idries Shah, Jonathan Cape, paperback by Picador.

The Use of Lateral Thinking, The Mechanism of Mind, Po – Beyond Yes and No and *Practical Thinking* by Edward de Bono, the first three published in paperback by Penguin, and the last in hardback by Jonathan Cape, 1971.

Concentration and Meditation by Christmas Humphreys, Watkins, 1973 – the first part is the most useful in a dowsing context.

Zen and the Art of Motorcycle Maintenance by Robert M. Pirsig, Bodley Head, 1974.

Of these, the most important (to my mind) is *Zen and the Art of Motorcycle Maintenance*, for it demonstrates, in a very gentle way, a number of practical solutions for almost all the problems of approach and thought that are likely to turn up in dowsing – or any other situation, for that matter.

Medical and agricultural   *Radionics in Theory and Practice* by John Wilcox, Herbert Jenkins, 1960. Good coverage of the general principles of early radionics and some assorted variants, including the Colourscope and the Radionic Camera – but not much in the way of practical detail.

An Introduction to Medical Radiesthesia and Radionics, by Vernon D. Wethered, C. W. Daniel, 1957. A good general introduction, with a lot of practical detail on the use of a pendulum and ruler to supply number and proportion, rather than using a conventional radionic 'box'. Strong emphasis on the use of homeopathic remedies for treatment.

Radionics and the Subtle Anatomy of Man by David Tansley, Health Science Press, 1972. Best described as a manual for his 'Centre-Therapy' radionic box, using a system and approach which is deeply rooted in Hindu mystical theory. But although the material is clearly aimed at this specific use, its good mixture of practice and theory makes it easy to apply to other personal systems and uses.

Dowsing and archaeology *Pattern of the Past,* by Guy Underwood, Pitman, 1969; reissued in hardback by Museum and in paperback by Abacus. A lot of practical information, with a lot of detailed observations about dowsing-patterns which have since been checked by many other dowsers, including myself – but his theorizing seems a little suspect.

Mysterious Britain by Janet and Colin Bord, Garnstone, 1972, paperback by Paladin. A useful if somewhat superficial guide to the whole range of 'live' archaeology – a 'magical history tour', if you like. I particularly recommend it as a first book to read on the field, even though (or perhaps because) it doesn't really cover anything in detail.

The Old Straight Track by Alfred Watkins, Methuen, 1925; reissued in hardback by Garnstone, 1970, and in paperback by Abacus. This has almost no information on dowsing, but it is *the* classic piece of 'live' archaeology – and great fun to read, anyway. The implications of his 'ley' hypothesis from a dowsing point of view are more clearly explained in *Quicksilver Heritage* by Paul Screeton, Thorsons, 1974. Excellent coverage and extension of Watkins' original hypothesis from almost every angle (physical and non-physical), including dowsing. This I'd recommend as a second book, after *Mysterious Britain*, for anyone just starting on the field, rather than the more usual ones, John Michell's *View over Atlantic* (Garnstone, 1969) and Alexander Thom's *Megalithic Sites in Britain* (Oxford University Press, 1969). These last two books are excellent in their own ways, but I think require a prior knowledge of cabalistic or statistical practice and theory respectively to be much use from a dowsing point of view.

Organizations

The British Society of Dowsers. The present Secretary is Mr P. B. Smithett, 19 High Street, Eydon, Daventry, Northants. Membership is currently £6·00 a year, with a £1·00 entrance fee.

The Society has been going since 1936, has about 800 members all over the world, publishes an excellent quarterly Journal and organizes meetings, weekend conferences and other activities up and down the country. Unlike many 'fringe' organizations it does seem to know what it's doing, which I suspect is partly attributable to its lack of a fixed ideology (at a meeting one speaker will put forward one theory, the next speaker a completely incompatible one, but both will be taken seriously – which is something of a refreshing change!) Services to members include a good postal library, and the manufacture and sale of pendulums, whalebone rods, Mager discs, and other bits and pieces including a booklet, *Elementary Radiesthesia* by F. A. Archdale, which I personally find somewhat limited and confusing. The members as a whole are a practical bunch, and many will give friendly advice and instruction to beginners. But not all the members are practising dowsers, and anyone interested in dowsing and in 'the objects of the Society' may join.

Radionic Association, The Secretary, Field House, Peaslake, Guildford, Surrey. Membership currently £5·00 a year.

The Association is concerned almost exclusively with medical dowsing. It publishes a quarterly magazine, and organizes conferences, and holds courses on handling radionic instruments from a basic to professional level. The courses lead up to the Association's examination, after which the trainee is allowed to practise professionally.

Psionic Medical Society, Hindhead, Surrey.

Research and training in the direct application of dowsing in general to medicine, and to some extent to agriculture. Its approach is aimed mainly at the medical profession, though it does have a number of 'lay' members.

Research Into Lost Knowledge Organisation (RILKO) 36 College Court, Hammersmith, London W6.

RILKO is an academic research organisation which 'carries out impartial studies in a workmanlike way' on areas of information which don't seem to fit conventional prehistory. It publishes books, and collections of 'papers' by members such as Keith Critchlow, John Michell and Alexander Thom.

Another useful 'organization' is Paul Screeton's magazine-cum-information-exchange *The Ley Hunter*, which covers not only leys but also most other aspects of 'live' archaeology. The address is 5 Egton Drive, Seaton Carew, Hartlepool, Cleveland TS25 2AT; at present (1976) the magazine is bi-monthly, and costs 25p an issue or £1·50 subscription.

Manufacturers *The Omni-Detector Company*, 27 Latham Road, Twickenham, Middlesex.

This unlikely-sounding company manufactures an 'Omni-Detector Kit', a basic dowsing kit which costs around £4·00. The kit consists of a spring rod made of spring steel, a pair of simple angle rods, a 'short' and a 'long' pendulum (made of Perspex), and a basic manual – very basic, and rather confusing, in my opinion. The spring rod (again, in my opinion) is too weak as a spring to be of much use, but apart from that the kit is fairly good value for money, especially as a present to a prospective beginner.

De la Warr Laboratories, Raleigh Park Road, Oxford.

The late George de la Warr and his colleagues were the pioneers of radionics in this country – among other things they developed the extraordinary Radionic Camera, the radionic equivalent of an X-ray camera. They manufacture various types of 'box', for radionic diagnosis and treatment, and for research.

Metaphysical Research Group, Archer's Court, Stonestile Lane, Hastings, Sussex.

They manufacture and/or retail by mail order a wide range of dowsing equipment – pendulums, whalebone rods and the like – and other 'occult' equipment such as crystal balls. They also publish reprints of rare books – but their prices tend to be on the high side.

Bookshops   I don't know many bookshops out of London, but three well-established specialists in London are:

Watkins, 21 Cecil Court, Charing Cross Road, London WC2. A long-established shop where you can expect to be guided to the best books in the field. They have excellent stocks of both Eastern and Western mysticism, some second hand, and a good range of ecological books.

Compendium, 281 Camden High Street, London NW1. Originally a political and cultural bookshop, Compendium have expanded their range in recent years to include the 'fringe sciences' and 'alternative lifestyles'. They're particularly good for imported American books.

Atlantis, 49a Museum Street, London WC1. A delightful and friendly little shop near the British Museum, they specialize in magical and 'occultist' texts – some of which I've not seen anywhere else.